*The Continuing Legacy of the Scotch-Irish in America*

**ALISTER JOHN McREYNOLDS**

**COLOURPOINT BOOKS**

Published 2013 by Colourpoint Books
an imprint of Colourpoint Creative Ltd
Colourpoint House, Jubilee Business Park
21 Jubilee Road, Newtownards, BT23 4YH

Tel: 028 9182 6339

Fax: 028 9182 1900

E-mail: info@colourpoint.co.uk

Web: www.colourpoint.co.uk

First Edition
First Impression

Copyright © Colourpoint Books, 2013
Text © Alister J McReynolds, 2013
Illustrations © Various, as acknowledged in captions.

All rights reserved. No part of this publication may be reproduced, stored in a retrieval system or transmitted in any form or by any means, electronic, mechanical, photocopying, scanning, recording or otherwise, without the prior written permission of the copyright owners and publisher of this book.

The author has asserted his right under the Copyright, Designs and Patents Act, 1988, to be identified as author of this work.

A catalogue record for this book is available from the British Library.

Designed by April Sky Design, Newtownards
Tel: 028 9182 7195
Web: www.aprilsky.co.uk

Printed by GPS Colour Graphics Ltd, Belfast

ISBN 978-1-78073-040-0

*Rear cover:* Old McReynolds Homestead, Reeds Valley, Russell County, Virginia. A gift presented to the author by kinsman Lynn R Hawkins.

# CONTENTS

The Author .................................................... 5
Foreword ..................................................... 7
Introduction .................................................. 11
Chapter 1 – Reverend George Duffield *Chaplain of Congress and Advisor to George Washington, Ballymoney roots* ............... 13
Chapter 2 – Robert Adrain, Samuel Brown Wylie and John Fries Frazer *Three distinguished Ulster Academics in eighteenth century Pennsylvania* ........................................... 16
Chapter 3 – Reverend William Martin *1772, 5 ships and 467 families* 19
Chapter 4 – James Logan *Secretary of the Province of Pennsylvania* . . 22
Chapter 5 – Thomas Greg and Waddell Cunningham *All that is sweet may not be savoury* ................................... 25
Chapter 6 – James McHenry *The Ballymena man who became aide to George Washington* ......................................... 28
Chapter 7 – John Coffee Hays ................................... 31
Chapter 8 – General Andrew Thomas McReynolds ............. 35
Chapter 9 – Captain Jack Crawford *The Poet Scout, 1847-1917* ..... 39
Chapter 10 – General Sinclair Mulholland ..................... 46
Chapter 11 – Alexander Peter Stewart *Tennessee's highest ranking Confederate Officer* ........................................ 48

*Illustrations – Section One*

Chapter 12 – Samuel Sloan .................................... 50
Chapter 13 – Joseph Seamon Cotter Senior and Junior ......... 53
Chapter 14 – Scotch-Irish settlers in Southern Wisconsin ...... 56
Chapter 15 – Old Ripy Whiskey *Distilled by an Ulster family in the*

'Tyrone' distillery Kentucky . . . . . . . . . . . . . . . . . . . . . . . . . . . . . . . . . 59

Chapter 16 – Thomas Wolfe . . . . . . . . . . . . . . . . . . . . . . . . . . . . . . . 62

Chapter 17 – John Steinbeck *and his maternal Ulster–Scots family – the Hamiltons of Ballykelly* . . . . . . . . . . . . . . . . . . . . . . . . . . . . . . . 65

Chapter 18 – Clayton McMichen and Jimmie Rodgers . . . . . . . . . 69

Chapter 19 – Moon Mullican *Co–Writer of 'Jambalaya' and King of the Hillbilly Piano Players* . . . . . . . . . . . . . . . . . . . . . . . . . . . . . . . . . 72

Chapter 20 – Elvis Aaron Presley. . . . . . . . . . . . . . . . . . . . . . . . . . . . 75

Chapter 21 – Adlai Stevenson I and II *Grandfather and grandson* . . 79

*Illustrations – Section Two*

Chapter 22 – Wallace Hume Carothers *Inventor of Nylon* . . . . . . . . 82

Chapter 23 – Scotch–Irish settlement in New England . . . . . . . . . 85

Chapter 24 – The Rise and Fall of the McLellan family of Ballymoney and Maine . . . . . . . . . . . . . . . . . . . . . . . . . . . . . . . . . . . 95

Chapter 25 – Robert Dinsmoor *The picture painted with words in his poems and letters of Scotch-Irish pioneer settlement in New England* 100

Chapter 26 – Agents Temple and Dunbar *The work of 'Settlement Agents' in developing Scotch-Irish settlements in Maine* . . . . . . . . . . 108

Chapter 27 – Abolitionist Anthony Benezet quotes two Ulster Scots in support of his argument against slavery, but all may not be as it seems . . . . . . . . . . . . . . . . . . . . . . . . . . . . . . . . . . . . . . . . 113

Chapter 28 – Where Scotch-Irish history and culture can be visited in America today . . . . . . . . . . . . . . . . . . . . . . . . . . . . . . . . . 117

Acknowledgements. . . . . . . . . . . . . . . . . . . . . . . . . . . . . . . . . . . . . . 123

Index . . . . . . . . . . . . . . . . . . . . . . . . . . . . . . . . . . . . . . . . . . . . . . . . . . 124

# THE AUTHOR

Alister J McReynolds is the author of *Legacy, The Scots Irish in America* and also of *The Ulster Scots & New England*. Recently he has co-written a new Introduction to the 2012 publication, *Robert Dinsmoor's Scotch-Irish poems*.

McReynolds earned his MA at the University of Ulster, having gained his initial Bachelor's Degree and two post-graduate Diplomas from Queen's University, Belfast. He is currently an Honorary Research Fellow with the Centre for Irish and Scottish Studies at the University of Ulster and a Fellow of the Society of Antiquaries of Scotland.

McReynolds has spent over thirty years as a teacher in his native Province of Ulster, fourteen of those years being engaged as Principal of a Further Education College. He was awarded Honorary Membership of City and Guilds of London Institute as recognition of his contribution to vocational education in Northern Ireland. Currently he continues to lecture part-time with the Open Learning Department in Queen's University Belfast.

In the past five years McReynolds has lectured all over the United States including at the Smithsonian Institution in Washington DC. Nearer to home he was the presenter of this year's Ulster Scots Agency sponsored Whitelaw Reid Lecture in Belfast.

He lives with his wife Eileen and their family at Magheragall in Co Antrim.

**Grierson's Ride through Mississippi – Revisited**

*One October Sunday*
*Sunlight glinting sideways*
*Through the trunks*
*We drove through the woods*
*Missing birch poles by inches*
*To see the old family tannery*
*Famed for making boots*
*For the Confederacy,*
*Close by an old log house*
*Where four McReynolds brothers*
*Taught school*
*At different times*
*A hundred years ago or more,*
*We drove to the spot where Grierson*
*Came through*
*On his ride.*

*It's said that his troopers*
*Took no retribution*
*Because they were so well*
*Fed and watered,*
*Out here in rural*
*Oktibbeha County*
*Or cold bloody water*
*As it is in Choctaw*
*I expected to see*
*Wallsteads and buildings,*
*But instead find*
*Only the declivities*
*Of the tanning vats*
*Hollows bowls*
*Dried eye sockets*
*In the face of*
*The crumbly leafy earth.*

*Alister John McReynolds*

# FOREWORD

Some, though not all, of my research has been into the Scotch-Irish who settled in New England and particularly the group who made the State of Maine their home. Here in this Foreword, John Mann, who is Chair of the Maine Ulster-Scots Project (MUSP), tells us something about what it means to be of Scotch-Irish descent and living in Maine today.

*Alister J McReynolds*

## Foreword from America

Mainers prefer story-telling. Let's think about that. Meaghan, the daughter of a close friend, went 'away' to college. In Maine lingo, anyplace that's not Maine is 'away'. You're either a Mainer or you're from 'away'. It's a widely accepted fact. The cultural differences between Mainers and people from away can be as sharply defined as the Williamite and Jacobite armies facing each other across the Boyne. But, like so many things we're raised with, we don't always know what we know until someone who didn't know tells us. Meaghan's roommates at college told her, "no matter what we're discussing it always reminds you of a story".

Mainers prefer story-telling. We can exaggerate to make our point or add humor. We can understate to pry open the listener's imagination or add humor. We need to add enough fact to grab the listener's serious attention but the truth is not the primary objective. The story and the lesson it conveys is everything. Sarcasm is a formidable tool to be used without mercy. The story is alive and so it needs to be nourished with repeated tellings over time, over generations. The stories Mainers tell have legs and are handed down, inspected, improved on and shared at family gatherings. The embedded humor can be used for relief in times of stress, at funerals, and for plain old home-grown entertainment. Our character is shaped and reinforced by the stories that we preserve and share.

Maine story-telling is a great thing and we certainly enjoy it. Our story-telling, nowadays, is often marketed as 'Maine humor'. Did I mention the humor? An entire industry has been created out of 'Maine humor'. You can 'google' up a Maine humor story on the Internet anytime. Some are real classics. Some are so phony that they're an embarrassment to the tradition.

There is, of course, a point here. The history of Maine's Ulster-Scots (aka Scots-Irish, Scotch-Irish, etc) is primarily an oral history. It is full of humor, sarcasm, contempt and the celebration of idiosyncratic behavior. It reflects both who we are and who we were. The down-side is that the Ulster-Scots who settled Maine and defended America's eastern frontier have virtually no written history. Their written history, until recently, has been relegated to an occasional footnote in Maine history books. There was little time in frontier life for writing, but the oral tradition has endured. The written history of Maine has focused primarily on important events from the perspective of our Puritan neighbors to the south without attempting to document or tell the story of Maine's Presbyterian-based founding families. This is understandable and even justifiable at a certain level. In fact it may have been a service to Maine in the long run since it did not add an unnatural slant to the Maine Scots-Irish story. But ignoring the historical facts is not the solution either. Oral tradition alone will not save the facts for posterity.

In the introduction to *They Change Their Sky; the Irish in Maine*, Maine's former US Senator, and international peace broker, George Mitchell, stated it this way:

> *My work for peace in Northern Ireland has taught me that historical amnesia never succeeds in the long term and, therefore, it is imperative to chronicle the experience of this group ... especially as they represent the very first wave of Irish settlers in Maine.*

Since 2005 it has been the mission of the Maine Ulster-Scots Project (MUSP) to save and share the stories of Maine's first Scots-Irish families. In studying and evaluating their history we find ourselves examining certain features that motivated and supported the culture, and that have endured in our modern identity as Mainers. In a broad sense, these features are Family, Faith and Freedom.

- Family was very inclusive. Family reached out in all directions for four generations and it was expected to give the support needed for success in a hostile frontier environment. Family history and cultural identity was preserved through story telling and music.

- Faith was a constant guidepost and a tangible living thought that evolved of necessity over time from a geographically remote Presbyterian base to a local frontier Baptist religion. That newly-formed Baptist perspective spear-headed the push for independence from Massachusetts and eventual statehood for Maine in 1820.
- Freedom started with owning land. With clear land titles the Ulster emigrants could be free from rent payments, free to support themselves, free from the schemes of absentee land-lords and empire builders. They could have a freedom built on sweat equity, individual liberty, and family support. Their version of freedom was far removed from the social ordinances of Puritan Massachusetts and the central authority of an English monarchy.

An oral story-telling tradition is not unique to Maine, of course. It is a central part of the music that travelled with, and evolved from, the 'Scotch-Irish' migrations through Pennsylvania, down the Appalachian Mountains, and into America's south and west. Alister J McReynolds includes this element of the Ulster emigrant's story in his *Kith and Kin: the Continuing Legacy of the Scotch-Irish in America*. He has also chosen several Maine related stories. You will learn from the Maine based stories that where a family settled in relation to the Kennebec River had an enormous impact on their resulting success.

The Ulster families that were settled east of the Kennebec River by Dunbar, Temple and others, struggled for a century with the poverty and uncertainty resulting from challenged land titles. They had no freedom from absentee land-lords or Massachusetts-based empire builders. They were ultimately forced to mount their own back-woods revolution of 'liberty men' and 'white Indians' in order to clear the title to their homesteads.[1]

Families like the McLellans of Gorham and Falmouth, towns lying west of the Kennebec River, were able to purchase land titles that were not in disputed territory. Their resulting freedom, coupled with their Christian charity for the Native Americans led to substantial financial success. Their oral family stories were captured in writing by a descendant, Reverend Elijah Kellogg, and so have endured to be examined in relation to the larger Ulster-Maine emigration story.

---

1 "Widespread in mid-Maine, the settlers resistance (to proprietary land claims) began in the 1760s. Initially the insurgents called themselves 'Liberty Men' ... But their foes called them 'White Indians' ... on account of their disguises and their supposed savagery." Alan Taylor, *Liberty Men and Great Proprietors, The Revolutionary Settlement on the Maine Frontier, 1760–1820*, The University of North Carolina Press, 1990.

The Dinsmoor family first settled in the heart of the Kennebec River valley and was driven out by the Indian Raid of 1722. Their story represents the 'hot molten center' of the territorial disputes that occurred during the Indian Wars.

Together these stories help to explain why the Kennebec River Valley is central to the current investigative work of the Maine Ulster-Scots Project. Our on-going archaeological studies along the Kennebec River at Merrymeeting Bay and our continuing archival research of Maine's first Ulster families is bringing us ever closer to understanding the relationship between the Kennebec valley in Maine and the Bann valley in Northern Ireland. This work will help save the facts of our shared history and perhaps even add a written chapter to our Maine history books.

In continuing our work of 'Saving and Sharing Maine's Scots-Irish Heritage' some will ask, why is this important? I'll share with you Chip Griffin's perspective. Carl R 'Chip' Griffin III lives in the heart of Maine's mid-coast at Boothbay Harbor. Chip is an historian, author, and member of the Maine Ulster-Scots Project research team. He has studied, lectured and written extensively on Maine's Scotch-Irish pioneers. Chip states the relevance of our local Ulster-Scots heritage this way:

*We are who preceded us. Once we understand this concept, learn about our predecessors, and piece together some of this puzzle, we can then assemble a more clear, coherent, and colorful portrait of our own age, our towns, and ourselves. We can then live more fully in the present and even, perhaps, reach out to make a difference for those who follow.*

We hope you enjoy these stories and have the opportunity to visit Maine and learn more about our oral traditions, and our Ulster connections. What makes Maine unique is our people. The stories of our people are woven out of the legacy of Ulster.

For more information on the Maine Ulster-Scots Project you may visit our website at www.maineulsterscots.com or 'Like' us on Facebook.

Maine Ulster-Scots is a Project of the Saint Andrews Society of Maine www.mainehighlandgames.org

*John T Mann*
*Professional Land Surveyor*
*Chairman of the Maine Ulster-Scots Project*

# INTRODUCTION

Although this book is written in what I hope is a modest way, as a collection of life stories, the chain that binds these stories carries in its strength a serious purpose. The purpose is to persuade readers that the Scotch-Irish contribution to life in America was, and is, more valuable and less of a cliché than the images of rascality, motor sports and corn liquor suggest. But where was the evidence for my persuasive purposes? The answer is that it was not difficult to find. It was like mining in a disused mine where the nuggets were lying all around.

Firstly, others had written about the Scotch-Irish and Education. James G Leyburn had noted that, in early Scotch-Irish pioneer settlements, "schoolmasters were eagerly sought after in all communities." Ron Chesepiuk's observations about Scotch-Irish clergy point to a search for rigorous and intellectual leadership on the frontier, "Each Presbyterian Minister had to be a University graduate who had undergone a rigorous training period, which included the study of Greek, Latin, and Hebrew." I hope that people here in Ulster and Scotch-Irish people in America will be persuaded to recognise how much they have in common and the true nature of their heritage.

John Shelton Reed, Professor Emeritus and co-founder of the Center for the Study of the American South, presents a very telling picture of this lack of self-appreciation,

> "You ask people what their ethnicity is, and a lot of Scotch-Irish people either don't know or if they know it they just (don't) acknowledge it. It's not something they really identify with. They're just plain old Americans, plain vanilla."

However, the irony is that their contribution is perhaps so all-pervasive, that people don't notice it at all.

The Appalachian novelist Ron Rash, in a revealing note to this author, put it well:

> *Certainly the Scotch-Irish have had a huge impact on a number of different groups in the US, here in my Appalachian region the Scots-Irish influence is, by far, the predominant one – music, language and for sure spunk …*

Finally, in this book I have told the stories of some of my McReynolds kinsfolk as part of the overall picture. This has given me the title, *Kith and Kin*, which is, like so much Lowland Scots usage, Old English. In terms of meaning it is a collective term for, 'relatives and neighbours'. Robert Burns used the term often, most notably in his 1787 song, *My Lord A-Hunting*:

> *My lady's white, my lady's red,*
> *And Kith and Kin o'Cassillis blude,*
> *But her ten-pund lands o'tocher gude;*
> *Were a' the charms his lordship lo'ed.*

The lives portrayed in this book are not those of Lordships, nor those related to the noble Kennedys of Cassillis. On the other hand, they are not a group of people who were unremarkable, but rather a people who were achievers and just the kind of folk you would choose to lay the foundations of a new world.

*Alister J McReynolds*
*County Antrim, June 2013*

# CHAPTER 1

## Reverend George Duffield

*Chaplain of Congress and Advisor to
George Washington, Ballymoney roots*

Rev George Duffield was a key advisor to George Washington and a 'New Light' Presbyterian preacher, proclaimer and missionary. His roots lay in the County Antrim town of Ballymoney. His antecedents are believed to have been Huguenot with the family name being originally pronounced as 'Du Fielde'.

His father, also named George Duffield, was born in Ballymoney in 1690 and died in 'Duffield Place', Salisbury, Lancaster County, Pennsylvania in 1774. That George (it was to become a family Christian name just as, in America anyway, being a Presbyterian clergyman was to become a favourite family profession) emigrated in 1732 and bought substantial land and property in present day Lancaster County, Pennsylvania, near the Pequea township some 12 miles south of Lancaster. It was in that same year that his son George, the future Continental Congress chaplain, was born. He was educated initially at Newark Academy Delaware and following the well-worn path to the Presbyterian ministry, he progressed to Princeton where he duly graduated in 1752. Duffield was ordained in September 1761 and was firmly in the New Light Presbyterian faction, which included Jonathan Edwardes and George Whitefield. That year he became a minister shared by three congregations: Carlisle and Big Spring Newville, both in Cumberland County, Pennsylvania, and Monaghan Church in Dillsburg, York County. 'Dillsburg' was named after the Dill family, who were originally from Monaghan in Ulster. They settled in Pennsylvania early in the 1730s when many Scotch-Irish flooded into the area.

In September 1766 he completed a missionary tour through the valleys of Pennsylvania, Maryland and Virginia. This was aimed at conversion of Native Americans and took Duffield as far west as Ohio.[1] The tour was organised by

Rev Francis Allison who was happy to deploy Duffield in the role. However, as an 'Old Light' Presbyterian he differed fundamentally with Duffield's New Light thinking and preaching. This rift in ideology in American Presbyterianism resulted in an incident some five years later when George Duffield was given charge of the Third Presbyterian Church in Philadelphia, which is still today sometimes referred to as 'Old Pine Street Church'.[1] Duffield's suitability to fulfil this role was opposed by the Old Light Presbyterians. Arriving one Sunday to preach the sermon as usual he found that the Church door had been barred against him. Not to be outdone or denied, he is thought to have entered instead through an open window. At that point James Bryant, who was employed by the distinctly Old Light First Presbyterian Church as a magistrate, arrived and informed the gathered congregation that they were guilty of being illegally assembled. A member of the 'Old Pine' congregation, aptly named Robert Knox, with all the fervour of his namesake, the Scottish Reformer John Knox, summarily ejected the magistrate and then casually encouraged Rev Duffield to proceed with his sermon.[2] Ultimately the Revolutionary War intervened and removed much of the appetite for that particular theological fight. It is worth remembering that Philadelphia would have been at the heart of this controversy. There is a contemporary misconception that in the eighteenth century Philadelphia would have been predominately Quaker. In reality, since as early as 1739, Presbyterians outnumbered all other religious groups in the town.

Like many Scotch-Irish Presbyterians, Duffield used his position and pulpit to encourage his friends and congregation to support the American or 'Patriot' cause in the War of Independence.[3] Amongst those who heard him combine Revolution and the Gospel into a heady mixture of rhetoric was John Adams, who attended services there on occasions, including one on 17 May 1776. In a sense Adams, as a New England Congregationalist, may have been sceptical of Presbyterian adherence to the 'Patriot Cause'. However on that particular morning, as Adams wrote to his wife Abigail, Duffield preached a sermon which likened George III's treatment of Americans to Pharaoh's treatment of the Israelites.[1] He commented that he found Duffield to be "a man of genius and eloquence" and at another sermon he commented, "he filled and swelled the bosom of every hearer." The actual building of 'Old Pine', like many churches in war-time, suffered damage during the War. It was used as a hospital and the pews were used as body stretchers and firewood.

On 1 October 1777, the Continental Congress, which was meeting in Pennsylvania, voted to have more than one chaplain at a time, since their first incumbent in the role had deserted their cause and joined the British side. Two 'non-traitorous' chaplains, with Philadelphian flocks, were appointed –

William White, rector of Christchurch, Philadelphia and George Duffield, pastor of the Third Presbyterian Church. In this role, Duffield shared in the privations and dangers of the Continental Army to such an extent that he was particularly hated by the enemy. Consequently, they placed 'a price on his head'.

The role that was played in the Revolution by Scotch-Irish advisors is well seen in the comment made by Rev JH Bryson of Huntsville, Alabama, as recorded in the 'Proceedings of the Third Congress at Louisville', which looked at the role of 'Scotch-Irish influence upon the Formation of the Government of the United States':

> *Washington knew the value of these distinguished men as counselors, Witherspoon, Rodgers, McWhirter, Caldwell and Duffield were often in conference with him in the darkest days of the Revolution ... He knew he had their sympathies and he had respect for their judgment.*[4]

Reading the comments today, it is no wonder that George Washington felt that he would make his last stand amongst such persons if necessary.

After the War of Independence George Duffield focussed more closely on those duties associated with his original vocation. This focus culminated in his appointment as Clerk of the General Assembly. In his lifetime he published just two works, *An Account of a Missionary Tour through Western Pennsylvania in 1766* and a *Thanksgiving Sermon on Peace*, which was delivered on 11 December 1783. He died in Philadelphia on 2 February 1790.

# Endnotes

1. 'Biography – The Reverend George Duffield', Presbyterian Heritage Centre website, www.phcmontreat.org/bios/Duffield-George.htm, date accessed 22 April 2013
2. 'Old Pine Street Presbyterian Church', ushistory.org website, www.ushistory.org/tour/old-pine-presbyterian.htm, date accessed 22 April 2013
3. 'The Old Pine Story', Old Pine Street Church website, www.oldpine.org/history/the-old-pine-story, date accessed 22 April 2013
4. Rev JH Bryson, DD, of Huntsville, Alabama, 'Scotch-Irish influence upon the Formation of the Government of the United States' in *The Scotch-Irish in America, Proceedings of the Third Congress at Louisville*, Electric Scotland website, http://www.electricscotland.com/history/scotsirish/congress3-16.htm, date accessed 12 June 2013

# CHAPTER 2

## Robert Adrain, Samuel Brown Wylie and John Fries Frazer
*Three distinguished Ulster Academics in eighteenth century Pennsylvania*

Given the number of immigrants from Ulster who poured into America through the city of Philadelphia and the state of Pennsylvania, in the late eighteenth century, it is perhaps not all that surprising that a significant tranche of this well-educated group eventually found positions teaching in the University of Pennsylvania. What is surprising is that within a relatively short space of time at least three of these migrants should rise to occupy the post of Vice-Provost within its hierarchy.

Robert Adrain (often misspelled as 'Adrian') occupied the position from 1828 until 1834. He was born in Carrickfergus on 30 September 1775. His father was a French Huguenot, who had settled in Ulster after the Revocation of the Edict of Nantes, when French Protestants fled from oppression in their own country. In Carrickfergus, Adrain senior gained employment as a schoolteacher and as someone who made mathematical instruments.

Robert Adrain's parents died when he was just 15 years old and he was left to support himself and his four siblings. Even at that young age he displayed a remarkable ability with Mathematics and began to teach in Ballycarry, County Antrim. In that role he had acquired enough resource by the year 1798 to enable him to marry Ann Pollock. 1798 was also the year of the Rebellion of the United Irishmen, and Robert Adrain was actually employed by a British army officer as a tutor when hostilities broke out. Notwithstanding that, however, Robert joined the United Irishmen insurgents and received a bad wound to his back, which was inflicted accidentally by one of his 'brothers in arms'. Soon after he recovered, he and his young wife fled to America, where he taught in an Academy in Princeton, New Jersey for three years. In the period 1809–1813 he became Principal of York County Academy before moving on to a post as Principal of Reading Academy. University life beckoned, however, and Adrain was appointed as Professor of Mathematics and Natural Philosophy at Queen's College (or Rutgers College as it is now called). It was there that an Honorary LLD was conferred on him. In 1813 he resigned in order to take up a similar Chair in Columbia University. Robert Adrain remained in that post for a further 13 years and then returned to Rutgers for a year before being elected as Professor of Mathematics at the University of Pennsylvania in 1827. There he remained for a further seven years. In the period before his death, Robert Adrain published a number of seminal works. He died in New Brunswick in New Jersey on 10 August 1843. One of his seven children, Garnett B Adrain, was a Democratic member of the United States Congress from 1857 until 1861.[1]

The man who succeeded Adrain in his position as Vice-Provost at the University of Pennsylvania was Samuel Brown Wylie, who was born in Moylarg near Ballymena, County Antrim on 21 May 1773. Wylie was a graduate of the University of Glasgow in 1797 and taught for a short time in Ballymena. However, like Robert Adrain he supported the United Irishmen in the Rising and was compelled to take flight to America in 1797 on the eve of the Rebellion.

Having taken flight in such circumstances, Wylie had little difficulty in obtaining a teaching position in Cheltenham Pennsylvania. There he remained for the rest of 1797 before moving to the University of Pennsylvania in 1798, the year of the Great Rebellion itself.

Wylie also began studying reformed Presbyterian theology and followed the teachings of the Reformed or Covenanter faith in America. By 1799 he was licensed to preach within the denomination and three years later returned home as a delegate to a convention of the Reformed church in Scotland and Ireland.

Back in the United States he was appointed as Pastor of the First Reformed Presbyterian Church in Philadelphia. He held that position for most of half a century. For a time he also occupied the Chair of Languages in the University of Pennsylvania, of which he was Vice-Provost from 1838 until 1845.

Wylie was married to Margaret Watson of Pittsburgh whose family were first generation Scottish Americans. He died at his Philadelphia residence on 13 October 1852.[2]

John Fries Frazer was Vice-Provost of the University of Pennsylvania from 1855 until 1868. However, unlike two of his predecessors who are portrayed here, he was born in Philadelphia, not Ulster, on 8 July 1812. His great-great-grandfather John Frazer had been born in Ulster, of Scottish parents and had made his way to Philadelphia in 1735. There he had become a wealthy West

Indies shipping merchant. John Fries Frazer received his early education at a school in Germantown, then for one year at Captain Partridge's Military Academy in Connecticut. The thread, which runs through and connects those three men, can be seen here once again, as the young Frazer then went to stay with Rev Samuel Brown Wylie, who educated him at home. Wylie could have been proud of his skill as a pedagogue when his pupil became Professor of Chemistry and Physics the University of Pennsylvania. However, it was some three years after Wylie's death that John Fries Frazer became Vice-Provost of the same University. John Fries Frazer died suddenly of a heart attack on 12 October 1872.[3]

## Endnotes

1. 'Robert Adrian (1775–1843)', Pennsylvania University Archives & Records Centre website, www.archives.upenn.edu/people/1700s/adrain_robt.html, date accessed 23 April 2013
2. 'Samuel Brown Wylie', Pennsylvania University Archives & Records Centre website, www.archives.upenn.edu/people/1700s/wylie_saml_brown.html, date accessed 23 April 2013
3. 'Frazer Family, Papers, 1779–1955, 1977–1979', Pennsylvania University Archives & Records Centre website, www.archives.upenn.edu/faids/upt/upt50/frazerfam.html, date accessed 23 April 2013

## References

*Dictionary of American Biography*, Charles Scribners' Sons, New York, 1946

# CHAPTER 3

## Reverend William Martin

*1772, 5 ships and 467 families*

In the early eighteenth century, South Carolina had an extensive range of economic activity and settlement along the length of its coast. Much of this development was built around the cultivation of rice and depended heavily on the use of slave labour. State authorities and business developers realised it would be advantageous to build settlements which extended inland, where the soil suited other crops that were not dependant on the use of slave labour. From as early as 1731, 'poor Protestants' were offered land if they came to settle in the state. The usual package on offer was 100 acres to each head of family and 50 acres for every person in the family. Tools and provisions to work and sustain initial settlement were often provided free of charge and although there were requirements about clearing land, this was usually reasonably based on what was feasible over a generously calibrated period of time.

So, who was the Rev William Martin who organised Ulster-Scots to take advantage of this offer? William Martin was born on 16 May 1729, the eldest son of David Martin of Ballyspollum, near Ballykelly in County Londonderry. He was educated at the University of Glasgow and licensed to preach by the Reformed Presbyterian (Covenanter) Church at The Vow, County Antrim. Although the Reformed Presbytery had consolidated in Ulster as early as 1743, it was not until this event some 14 years later that they had a steady missionary preacher. William Martin later became heavily involved in encouraging and ordaining other Covenanter ministers. In 1760 he was living at Kellswater and preaching on a regular circuit at Cullybackey, Leymore, Cloughmills and Dervock, as well as Londonderry and continuing at The Vow Congregation, where he was originally ordained.

In 1770 he first received a 'call' to South Carolina and heeded it in 1772, taking 467 families on five ships with him. On one of these ships, *The Lord Dunluce,* Martin is listed as a passenger and as emigration agent. Not only were these Ulster-Scots attracted by the generous land grants but they also felt increasingly alienated in Ulster by high rents, paying tithes and poor business results. *The Lord Dunluce* sailed out of Larne on 4 October. It encountered contrary winds and did not reach Charleston, South Carolina until 2 December. During the journey 10 men and several children died of smallpox. As a result, the ship was quarantined for 15 days when it arrived at Charleston. Another of the five ships, *The James and Mary,* lost five children to smallpox and was quarantined for seven weeks just off Sullivan's Island adjacent to the South Carolina coast.

This area of South Carolina already had Presbyterian settlers, some from Ulster and others from neighbouring states. Within Craven County (now Chester Country) these settlers had built a church and they called it 'Catholic' to recognise its voluntary coalition of various forms of Presbyterianism to worship. The present day church on this site was built in 1842 and is the third building to accommodate the congregation. There is also a granite marker which was erected in 1933 to commemorate the 62 soldiers from the church who fought for the Patriot cause in the American Revolution. It was to this Presbyterian Fellowship that William Martin received the 'call' in 1770, two years before the exodus from Ulster.

Given the large number of people (467 families) it was impossible for all of those who sailed to get land close together, although many settled in the Rocky Mountain area, near Abbeville, where their leader made his home. A cursory examination of an old map of the area betrays the extent of Scotch-Irish settlement through the names of creeks and mills; Pattersons, Johnsons, Wilsons, McCords, McCaws and McKinleys all feature around Abbeville and the small town of Richburg.

At first Rev Martin preached at 'Catholic' regularly until, in 1774, the Covenanters withdrew from the church and built their own log church on the same road as 'Catholic' but two miles to the east of it.

Rev Martin had encouraged all Presbyterians in the area to support the American cause in the Revolution against Britain. For this he was incarcerated for several months and brought before British commander Lord Cornwallis, who released him on condition that he did not return to the County. Martin took refuge in North Carolina but returned to Chester County after the Revolution. He began preaching again at 'Catholic', since the Covenanters' log church been razed to the ground during the conflict.

After the Revolution many Covenanters and other Presbyterians began to express their hatred of slavery and in 1800 the Reformed Presbytery of the Covenanting Church unanimously banned members of its congregations from owning slaves. Two young clergy were sent from Ulster to enforce this ruling, namely the Rev Samuel Wylie, who is portrayed in the previous chapter, and the Rev James McKinney. These two clergy had been officially empowered by the church to excommunicate any members who felt unable to liberate their negro slaves. Thereafter, the majority of those who liberated slaves on this occasion moved to the North Western states.

Wylie and McKinney, as Commissioners, had another difficult task to perform and that was the suspension of Rev James McGarrah and the summary deposing of Rev William Martin, who was thus dealt with in spite of his evangelical and pioneering work in both Ulster and South Carolina. Many members of the congregation felt that two very inexperienced clergy had been asked to remove someone who was now aged nearly 72 and had been preaching for more than 45 years. His 'crime' was described as 'intemperance' although he, and others, claimed that it was simply his lifelong practice to accept a glass of whiskey when offered such hospitality at any house where he was making a visitation.

Notwithstanding this sanction, the Rev Martin continued to preach and was much in demand at school houses and meetings in private houses. In 1804 his stone house burned down and he built a modest log cabin near Richburg, where he lived for his few remaining years. In 1806 he fell off his horse and contracted a fever of which he died, and was buried in a small graveyard near his cabin. One biographical account describes him as "a large fine looking man, a proficient scholar, an eloquent preacher, and an able divine."

# Reference

Jean Stephenson, *Scotch-Irish Migration to South Carolina, 1772 (Rev William Martin and his five shiploads of Settlers)*, 1971

# CHAPTER 4

## James Logan

*Secretary of the Province of Pennsylvania,
Chief Justice, Mayor of Philadelphia, Commissioner of Property,
President of the Council and two years Governor of the Province*

The name Logan is derived from a locality and first occurs in Scottish history during the reign of William the Lion. The chief of the family was the Baron of Restalrig and one member of the family was married to a daughter of King Robert II. Sir Robert Logan and Sir William Logan were chief associates of Sir James Douglas, a Scottish commander during the Scottish Wars of Independence. In 1400 Sir Robert Logan of Restalrig was Lord Admiral of Scotland and defeated the English fleet at the Firth of Forth.

The family's estates were confiscated as a result of their involvement in the Gowrie affair.[1] Two of the sons of the family fled to Lurgan, County Armagh. Robert, the younger son, subsequently returned to Scotland and settled there. His son Patrick was educated for a career as a clergyman and gained an MA from the University of Edinburgh. He served for a time as a chaplain but relinquished his profession and returned to Ulster, where he joined the Society of Friends. Before he had left Scotland, Patrick married Isobel Hume, who was related to the Laird of Dundas and the Earl of Panmure. Patrick worked as a schoolteacher in Lurgan and had several children, but only William, who became an eminent physician in Bristol, and James survived.[2]

James was born in Lurgan in 1674 or 1675 and was thus the great-grandson of Sir Robert Logan, Baron of Restalrig.[3] He proved to be a great scholar from an early age and was well-versed in Latin, Greek and Hebrew before he was 13 years old. By age 16 he was very distinguished as a mathematician. At that stage James was apprenticed to a linen draper in Dublin but during the Williamite Wars he returned to Edinburgh, then London and Bristol. He became a teacher and greatly improved his knowledge of Greek and Hebrew, as well as learning French, Italian and Spanish.[2]

In the spring of 1699, James Logan was solicited by William Penn, who was very impressed by the young man, to accompany him to his newly founded colony in America. It was a three month journey and luckily so, as had they arrived earlier they may have suffered from the yellow fever which was raging through the Province just before their arrival.[2]

Logan had a number of administrative functions and William Penn came to have complete confidence in his abilities. Thus it is no surprise that he occupied so many prestigious positions in Pennsylvania.

Logan knew well the merits of the Ulster-Scots people, being one himself, albeit a Quaker.[2] As the Moira memorial demonstrates, he had Presbyterian relatives. We are told that he was a cousin of William Tennant, a famous clergyman from County Armagh who emigrated in 1718 and later founded 'The Log College', which eventually grew into Princeton University and crucially provided education and clerical training for Presbyterian ministers in America, who had previously had to journey to Glasgow for such purposes.

Logan knew the strength of the Ulster-Scots as frontiersmen and described in his diary how he set out around 1720 to deliberately plant settlements of these tough neighbours and friends from back home in Ulster:

> *At the time we were apprehensive from the Northern Indians ... I therefore thought it might be prudent to plant a settlement of such men who formerly had so bravely defended Londonderry and Inniskillen(sic) as a frontier in case of any disturbance ... these people if kindly used will be orderly as they have hitherto been and easily dealt with.*

And come they did! In the early eighteenth century almost 250,000 people left the north of Ireland and sought a new life in North America.

Logan felt he had opened the floodgates much wider than he had initially anticipated. He stated, "It looks as if Ireland is to send all her inhabitants thither, for last week no less than six ships arrived, and every week two or three arrive also".[4] He became somewhat concerned about possibly losing Quaker influence as a result, "If the Scotch-Irish continue to come they will make themselves masters of the Province".[5] And arguably they did just that, although the majority were passing through, heading for lands in Ohio and Virginia and down the Great Wagon Road.

Logan's home in Philadelphia is a magnificent colonial mansion called 'Stenton', which he built in 1728 in Germantown. It has been restored and is now an historic building open to the public.[2]

Logan was a friend and mentor to Benjamin Franklin, who had the privilege of printing many of his scientific papers in the fields of Botany and

Optics. He made a considerable fortune from the fur trade and from land investments. For one who was such a scholar and who gave 3,000 volumes to the City of Philadelphia, which formed the basis of the Loganian Library,[6] it seems only fitting that the James Logan High School was named after him. He was also one of the founders and trustees of the Academy of Pennsylvania, now known as the University of Pennsylvania.[3]

The Moira branch of the family embellished the gravestone in Moira Presbyterian churchyard with their justifiable pride at being the relative of such an illustrious man. They chiefly resided at Church Hill, Trummery on the outskirts of the village.

## Endnotes

1. James Grant, 'Old and New Edinburgh', Vol 5, Cassell and Company Limited, www.oldandnewedinburgh.co.uk/volume5/page144.html, date accessed 24 April 2013
2. 'The Life of James Logan', ushistory.org website, www.ushistory.org/penn/jameslogan.htm, date accessed 24 April 2013
3. 'James Logan (1674–1751)', Pennsylvania University Archives & Records Centre website, www.archives.upenn.edu/people/1700s/logan_jas.html, date accessed 24 April 2013
4. Wilson Armistead, *Memoirs of James Logan, A Distinguished Scholar and Christian legislator, including Several of his letters and those of his Correspondents*, 1851
5. 'The Scots-Irish of Tennessee', Tennessee Online website, http://www.tennesseehistory.com/class/ScotIrish.htm
6. 'James Logan', ushistory.org website, www.ushistory.org/germantown/people/logan.htm, date accessed 24 April 2013

## Reference

James G Leyburn, *The Scotch-Irish: a Social History*, University of North Carolina Press, 1962, p191

# CHAPTER 5

## Thomas Greg and Waddell Cunningham
*All that is sweet may not be savoury*

The Greg family originated in Ayrshire, in particular the village of Ochiltree, a few miles south of Kilmarnock. It is believed that they were Covenanters. In 1693, John, son of James Greg was born in Ochiltree. He worked in the village as a blacksmith before making his way to Belfast at 23 years old. John Greg had two sons: John, born in 1716 and Thomas, born in 1718. In time these brothers would develop easy relationships with the merchant houses of London and also with the banking fraternity within that city. John (junior) launched his first ship in the early 1740s, a brig named *The Greg*.

Waddell Cunningham was descended from Planter stock who had settled at Ballymacilhoyle, near where the International Airport stands today. He had built a business in Belfast, dealing in flaxseed with American merchants, particularly with New York. During the 'Seven Years War' (1756–1763), Cunningham became quite wealthy selling Irish provisions to British planters.

In September 1763 Thomas Greg's vessel, *The Lord Hertford*, laden with coal and timber opened the new navigation link between Belfast and Lisburn. He and his wife lavishly entertained those who had literally followed the voyage. The feast included:

> *cold collation and wines of all sorts in great perfection, besides a band of musick (sic), which played the whole way, to upwards of one thousand persons who accompanied the lighter on the banks of the canal up to the town of Lisburn, where the inhabitants ... had their windows completely (sic) illuminated and bonfires lighted in the marketplace.*[1]

After a period of business in London, Waddell Cunningham returned to Belfast in 1765 and entered into a new partnership with Thomas Greg. During that year Thomas Greg had opened a shop in Lisburn and the new partnership was to some extent built on that decision. As the *Belfast Newsletter* of 21 April 1767 tells us:

> In 1766 Greg and Waddell Cunningham set up their 'vitriol manufactory' on an island in the Lagan River at Lisburn, the town where Greg established a timber yard the following year.[2]

Both Thomas Greg and Waddell Cunningham were of Presbyterian persuasion but nonetheless they 'courted' the local Anglican aristocracy. Part of this 'courtship' was the bequeathing of names to lighters that thereby honoured and flattered the local aristocracy, such as the aforementioned *The Lord Hertford* (1763) and the *The Countess of Donegall* (1766). Both Greg brothers, Thomas and John, were close to Wills Hill, Earl of Hillsborough, who, as Colonial Secretary, appointed John to the 'plum' position of Secretary to the Commissioners for the Sale of Lands in islands ceded by France under the 'Treaty of Paris' which ended the war.

John Greg spent much time trading in the West Indies auctions of French plantations and in Dominica he renamed one former French plantation as 'Hillsborough' in honour of his mentor. It is worth stating that those estates were worked by slaves purchased from British slave ships. Indeed as this book, *Kith and Kin*, neared printing, the *Belfast Telegraph* published a feature[3] by local historian Raymond O'Regan, revealing that in 1786 several Belfast merchants called a meeting at the Exchange and Assembly Rooms, Waring Street, Belfast with the expressed agenda of exploring the possibility of creating a slave-ship company in the city. The article is quite specific in stating that "Cunningham [Waddel] and Thomas Gregg [alternate spelling] were the main architects of the scheme". It explains that both these parties had returned from New York, where they had been engaged in trade with the Caribbean. The itinerary of trade that was mooted was fourfold:

   a) Ship goods to the Gold Coast.[4]
   b) Purchase captured slaves.
   c) Deliver slaves to West Indian sugar plantations.
   d) Return to Belfast with cargoes of brandy and sugar.[5]

The grand plan was thwarted as a cumulative effort of "the attitude of many radical Presbyterians in Belfast." Particularly active in this humanitarian way was one Thomas McCabe who was a goldsmith and watchmaker in

North Street Belfast and who belonged to First Belfast, Rosemary Street Presbyterian Church.

O'Regan's article suggests that there was a radical Presbyterian community in Belfast at that time, which abhorred the entire concept of slavery. So much so that in 1791, Olaudau Equiano, a well-known freed slave, felt that it was a good place to publicise his book on his personal experiences of slavery. He is recorded as staying with the woollen draper and later United Irishman, Samuel Neilson. Many, but not all, radical Presbyterians who took an anti-slavery stance were later to be involved in the 1798 United Irishmen's Rebellion. The father of Henry Joy McCracken for instance is mentioned in the article as being "involved in trade with the West Indies but was never involved in the transportation of slaves".[3]

## Endnotes

1. *Belfast Newsletter*, 9 September 1763
2. *Belfast Newsletter*, 21 April 1767
3. Raymond O'Regan, 'Man who kept of the right side of slavery', *Belfast Telegraph*, 20 June 2013, http://www.belfasttelegraph.co.uk/opinion/news-analysis/man-who-kept-city-on-right-side-of-slavery-29359322.html, date accessed 28 June 2013
4. The Gold Coast was latterly a British colony on the Gulf of Guinea in West Africa, from which, initially the Portuguese, and then other European nations had been running slaves since the 15th Century. Today it is recognised as having existed within the boundaries of the modern independent nation of Ghana.

## Reference

Michael James, *From Smuggling To Cotton Kings: The Greg Story*, Memoirs, 2010, can be accessed at http://issuu.com/tonytingle/docs/9780956510228_content, date accessed 23 April 2013

'Hidden Connections: Slavery and Belfast', Culture Northern Ireland, www.culturenorthernireland.org/article/101/hidden-connections-slavery-and-belfast, date accessed 8 May 2013

# CHAPTER 6

## James McHenry

*The Ballymena man who became aide to George Washington*

James McHenry was born in Ballymena in 1753 and was the son of Daniel, a prosperous merchant whose family had by that time been settled in the town for many generations. Young James received a classical education in Dublin and was exceedingly fond of writing poetry. In 1771, at 18 years of age, he immigrated to America. There he continued his education at the Newark Academy in Delaware, a school founded and run by the brothers Rev Patrick and Rev Francis Allison. McHenry's father, along with Agnes his mother and younger brother John, came the following year and established a prosperous import-export business in Baltimore, Maryland. Agnes died in 1774, just two years after her arrival, aged 46.

In 1773 Daniel McHenry established a business, 'Daniel McHenry and Son', in Baltimore with younger son John. Newspapers of the day advertised goods from "London, Liverpool, Ireland" and listed in particular "Dry goods, cloths, hardware, groceries, spiceries, wines, teas, brandies". The store was situated on the east side of Calvert Street, south of Market, now Baltimore Street. Initially, James and his brother were very involved with the business, however, James was not content to settle. He left to spend two years as an understudy of the noted surgeon Benjamin Rush. Albeit, it was not just for his prowess as a medical man that Rush was renowned. He was also a leading voice in the call for the American colonies to separate from Britain. Rush was regarded as one of the leading political thinkers in the cauldron of dissent and revolution that the State of Pennsylvania resembled at that time. He was later to become one of the 'signers' of the Declaration of Independence and no doubt he imbued the young McHenry with many of these ideas.

When the American Revolution broke out in 1775, James McHenry had only been in America for four years and was still a civilian. He became involved when he joined the American forces in Boston, where he worked in the military hospital in Cambridge, Massachusetts as a volunteer assistant surgeon. In that first year of the Revolution, McHenry said he was determined "to defend the liberties of Americans and mankind against the enemies of both". Before long he was asked to take on the full-time role of surgeon in New York City, in one of the hospitals set up to care for the wounded in the event of an abortive attack on Canada. He did not hesitate and rushed quickly to Philadelphia to collect additional medical supplies before heading to New York.

Late in 1776, when he was on the staff of the Fifth Pennsylvania Battalion, McHenry was captured by British forces at Fort Washington, New York. He was paroled early the following year and 'exchanged' in March 1778. He returned to duty immediately and was assigned to Valley Forge, Pennsylvania. In May of that year he became Secretary and aide to General George Washington. This assignment took place just prior to the Battle of Monmouth. Due to the prominence that James' father Daniel had achieved as a merchant, he was able to intercede with other substantial Baltimore merchants and persuade them to provide supplies for Lafayette's army on its Virginia expedition. Also, due to his family's excellent financial circumstances at this time, McHenry was able to forsake the practice of medicine in favour of public life and never really needed to revert to his profession again. He remained as a member of Washington's staff until 1780, when he then became aide to the Marquis de Lafayette.

James McHenry was a 'signer' of the United States Constitution on behalf of Maryland and served in the Senate of that state, as well as representing the State in the Continental Congress, for a period concurrently. McHenry was one of three physicians involved in drafting the Constitution, with Hugh Williamson and James McClurg being the other two. In August 1787 James McHenry made notes of the debates. The constitutional historian Max Farrand described these as "quite the best", representing a useful addition to the official journal and to James Madison's *Debates*.

Notwithstanding his signature, James McHenry had considerable misgivings about the power given to the central government compared to that dispersed in the individual states. However, he stated that he believed that "the good to be derived from the new Constitution outweighs its deficiencies." Reporting to the Legislature on proceedings in the Convention he made the following remarks:

*I myself could not approve of it throughout, but I saw no prospect of getting a better. The whole however, is the result of that spirit of Amity which directed the wishes of all for the general good, and where those sentiments govern, it will meet I trust with a kind and cordial reception.*[1]

Washington made McHenry Secretary of War in January 1796 and he continued to hold the post during John Adams' Presidency, although the relationship with the latter was not as strong since McHenry favoured Adams' great rival, Alexander Hamilton. During his period as Secretary of War, McHenry struggled valiantly with the task of building up a disciplined standing army for the 'new' country. However, at the President's request McHenry resigned in May 1800.

So the Ballymena man returned to his estate near his adopted city of Baltimore and entered a period of semi-retirement, during which time he was President of the Bible Society. He died in 1816 aged 62 and was buried in Baltimore's Westminster Presbyterian Cemetery.

During James McHenry's lifetime Fort McHenry near Baltimore was named after him. As it transpired, his son participated as a wartime volunteer in the 1814 defence of the fort, during the fierce bombardment which inspired Francis Scott Key to write the 'Star-Spangled Banner' about this event of spirited defence, which came to be seen as symbolising the courage of America's defiance in the face of all who threatened its peace.

## Endnotes

1. Ed Max Farrand, 'James McHenry Before The Maryland House Of Delegates', in *The Records of the Federal Convention of 1787*, New Haven, Yale University Press, 1911, Vol 3

## Reference

'A Biography of James Henry', American History from Revolution to Reconstruction and Beyond website, http://www.let.rug.nl/usa/biographies/james-mchenry/, date accessed 24 April 2013

'James McHenry, Maryland', US Army Centre of Military History, www.history.army.mil/books/RevWar/ss/mchenry.htm, date accessed 24 April 2013

# CHAPTER 7

## John Coffee Hays

John Coffee Hays was one of the earliest of the Texas Rangers and played a major role in the history of Texas and California. His ancestor, also called John Hays, was a Donegal man, who was born in 1704 and married Jane Love (born 1712) in Ireland before emigrating from the Donegal/Londonderry area around 1730, following the emigrant trail prevalent at the time, to Pennsylvania. Ironically, when he died he was buried in Derry, Pennsylvania.

His son, Robert Hays, was the offspring of John Hays of Donegal by his second wife, Martha Thompson. Young Robert grew up in the Scotch-Irish Rockbridge County of Virginia and during the American Revolution he distinguished himself as a Lieutenant of Infantry. He eventually rose to the rank of Colonel and erected Fort Haysboro in Wilson County, Tennessee, some seven miles south of Nashville. He married into the Donelson family who 'built' the city of Nashville. His wife was Jane Donelson, whose sister Rachel married Andrew Jackson, later hero of the Battle of New Orleans, where he defeated the 'cream' of the British army, and indeed first of the Scotch-Irish Presidents of the United States. Robert's son Harnon married Elizabeth Cage and their son, John, was born at Little Cedar Lick right there in Wilson County on 28 January 1817.[1] Harnon fought with Andrew Jackson and Sam Houston in the War of 1812. Young John (Jack) Coffee Hays was a constant visitor at Jackson's home 'The Hermitage' and idolised his great-aunt Rachel. It was a big blow to him when she died.[2]

John Coffee Hays, Texas Ranger extraordinaire and later a prominent officer during the Mexican War, left home at 15 years of age and learned the skills of surveying lands, initially working as a 'chain-boy', in the state of Mississippi. He attended Davidson Academy in Nashville and as early as 1838, he and his brother William moved from Mississippi to Texas to work for Sam Houston as surveyors. The nature of this work in the open spaces of the Texas Hill country raised Native American suspicions and the Hays brothers became regular targets for Comanche attacks. It was there and during that period that John Coffee Hays learned the rudiments of his Indian fighting prowess.

On Sam Houston's advice, Hays joined a company of Texas Rangers under the leadership of Erastus Smith and in that role he built a considerable reputation. The unit engaged the Mexican Cavalry near Laredo and assisted in the capture of Juan Sanchez. Hays showed promise even at this early stage and rose quickly to the rank of Sergeant. In the ranks, Jack Hays was idolised by his men, becoming a Captain at 23, Major at 25, and Colonel at 31, and is still considered by some to have been the greatest Indian fighter in Texas history.

The Texas Rangers as citizen soldiers were characterised as having an original and 'macho' persona, wearing frontier clothing and carrying up to three pistols, often supplemented by a short rifle and a bowie knife.[3] They marched and fought with a notable lack of military discipline and performed their role as an irregular force in a manner which left a big imprint on Texan and American History. Although Jack Hays proved to be a strong leader and a fearless fighter who earned the respect of rank and file Texas Rangers, like Kit Carson he was 'willowy' and stood just 5 foot 9 inches. He had mild manners that were in no way stereotypical and a striking appearance, with dark hair and pale skin which suggested his Scotch-Irish ancestry.[3] In the period 1840–1846, when Jack rose from Captain to Major, he engaged Mexican troops and Comanche braves in various skirmishes and battles. At one battle, Enchanted Rock, he made a lone stand that made him a legend as an Indian fighter. At Salado and Walker's Creek he fought with considerable success against the immigrant General, Paris born Adrian Woll and his Mexican troops. Woll was later made a Companion of the Legion of Honour and died at Montauban, near Toulouse in Southern France, in February 1875. In virtually all those engagements Hays' men were outnumbered but managed to 'even up the score' by making considerable, and for that period revolutionary, use of revolvers.

When the Mexican War broke out Hays and his Texas Rangers proved their worth, if ever there was any doubt about it. Now Hays was a Colonel at the head of the 'First Regiment, Texas Mounted Riflemen,' and, serving under General Zachary Taylor, distinguished himself and his men in their encounters with Mexican guerrillas. Shortly thereafter their position was 'regularised' along more formal military lines and the Rangers were given the key role of keeping open communication lines between Vera Cruz and Mexico City, to provide safe passage for the troops of General Winfield Scott. To this day the Mexican people have bad memories of the excesses of these engagements on both sides.[4]

While still living in Texas, Jack Hays met and married Miss Susan Calvert, who was born in Huntsville Alabama but was one of the Baltimore Calverts who could trace their lineage to Lord Baltimore.

After the Mexican War Hays was determined to grab his share in the 'forty-niner' Gold Rush to California. Once there, he settled and made California his new home. Initially he was elected Sheriff of San Francisco County and went on to occupy several public offices, including Surveyor General of California.[4] He was a pragmatic, progressive sort of man and soon became involved in the founding of the city of Oakland in the San Francisco Bay area, eventually becoming its Mayor. He took a neutral position during the Civil War and in 1876 he was a delegate to the Democratic National Convention.

Jack Hays died on 1 April 1883. He was buried in Mountain View Cemetery, Oakland – the city he had made his own.[1]

## Endnotes

1. 'John Coffee "Jack" Hays, 1817–1883', Texas Ranger Hall of Fame and Museum website, http://www.texasranger.org/halloffame/Hays_John.htm, date accessed 24 April 2013
2. 'Tejano History: 1850 John Coffee Hays', Texas Tejano website, http://www.texastejano.com/history/john-coffee-hays/, date accessed 12 June 2013
3. 'A Brief History of the Texas Rangers', Texas Ranger Hall of Fame and Museum website, www.texasranger.org/history/BriefHistory1.htm, date accessed 24 April 2013
4. 'John Hays', Spartacus Educational website, www.spartacus.schoolnet.co.uk/WWhaysJ.htm, date accessed 24 April 2013

## Martinsburg Road

*Now at fifty three*
*I have trained*
*My men*
*Not to change forwards*
*As Kearney and I*
*And one hundred dragoons*
*Did at Churubusco.*

*Here in West Virginia*
*With massive brigade weight*
*Creaking and clanking*
*We up and leave*
*Campfire embers burning*
*Beans heating in the pot.*

*Yesterday they brought*
*A captured Reb. before me*
*'Where are you from?'*
*I asked him*
*'I'm from Dungannon*
*Like yourself sir'.*

Alister J McReynolds

# CHAPTER 8

## General Andrew Thomas McReynolds

Andrew Thomas McReynolds was born in Northland Row, Dungannon, on Christmas Day 1808. His obituary said that he always insisted that it was 1806 but his gravestone shows 1808 as the date. His mother's name was Ann Sloane and through her he was a full cousin of Andrew Jackson, the seventh President of the United States and the first of a long Presidential line to have origins on the island of Ireland. This accolade is often mistakenly bestowed on John Fitzgerald Kennedy.

Andrew McReynolds' grandfather, Anthony, was a renowned lawyer who had offices on Sackville Street (later O'Connell Street), Dublin and was Sheriff for County Tyrone in 1807 and again in 1814. Andrew's father John was also a distinguished member of the Irish bar. His mother Anne, who was born in 1779, later accompanied him to America and died there in Cherry Street, Grand Rapids, Michigan, aged 90.

Perhaps it was the motivation he derived from tales of his cousin Andrew Jackson's growing reputation, but whatever the reason, when his father John died, Andrew McReynolds converted his inheritance into a bag of gold and headed for America, landing first in New York. That was in 1830 and Andrew Jackson was President, having been elected to his first term in the White House in 1828. Another relative was Louis McLane, who was Secretary of Treasury and Secretary of State in Jackson's cabinet. McLane was also President of the Baltimore and Ohio Railroad. McReynolds stayed in Pittsburgh for just three years, before heading westwards and settling in Detroit in 1833 and Grand Rapids in 1859. He began his law practice in Detroit in 1840. When McReynolds arrived in Detroit it was then a relatively small town with just 2,500 of a population. Just four years after settling there he was elected as an Alderman for the city.[1]

Prior to leaving Pittsburgh, Andrew McReynolds had engaged in his first military activities. Predictably these were in support of President Jackson. A federal tariff had been imposed in 1828 and again in 1832, and it was believed by the citizens of South Carolina that Jackson would remove these tariffs when he came into office. Jackson, however, supported the tariffs and disagreed openly with his Vice President John C Calhoun, who was a Scotch-Irish statesman from South Carolina. When the South Carolina State Convention declared the tariffs 'unconstitutional' in late February 1833, military preparations were made to enforce the issue. McReynolds served with the Pittsburgh Company in that activity. In March 1833, the South Carolina Convention reconvened and repealed the tariff. The state of South Carolina had not been fully united behind the action.

In 1839 McReynolds was one of the delegates to the Harrisburg Convention, which nominated William Henry Harrison as candidate for President. Harrison was successful and took office in March 1841. Unfortunately his term of office was short-lived and he died after just 32 days in the White House, in April of that same year. It was the start of McReynolds' serious engagement with the Democratic Party, however, and in 1847 he became a Democratic member of the Michigan Senate. There his eloquent remarks on the subject of relations with Mexico so impressed President Polk that he tendered McReynolds a captaincy in the Third Michigan Dragoons. When McReynolds led a hundred of these Dragoons against 6,000 Mexican and San Patricio troops at Churubusco, they fought all the way to the walls of the citadel and swept all before them. Andrew was immediately promoted to Major in the field for his personal bravery.[2] He was badly wounded by grapeshot in his left arm in the engagement and the limb was rendered useless for the rest of his long life. Phil Kearney, who fought beside McReynolds in the rout, lost his arm in the action. Thereafter Kearney's style of horsemanship in battle involved holding his sword in his right arm and holding the reins of the horse in his teeth.[3]

After Andrew McReynolds returned to Detroit at the end of the Mexican War, he was presented with a magnificent jewelled sword. The cost had been met by public subscription with no individual being allowed to give more than ten cents to the collection. Years earlier, when there had been an outbreak of Asiatic cholera in Detroit, he had voluntarily nursed sick citizens back to health. In gratitude, the people of Detroit presented him with a large cameo pin, which he wore at his breast for the rest of his days. When he returned to Detroit, McReynolds also became the first Captain of the Montgomery Guard.

In 1859 he moved to Grand Rapids, Michigan and once again began to practice law. The Civil War broke out and at the personal solicitation of Abraham Lincoln he was invited to form a cavalry regiment. He did so in New York, where such was his reputation, that the fact that he was in charge was used on posters as an inducement to recruitment.

McReynolds served as Colonel of the First New York Cavalry and was brevetted to General in the field. One incident from the War is captured in the poem on page 34 and is this writer's 'take' on an incident during the Second Battle of Winchester, when McReynolds' troops were being pursued by Jubal Early, who commanded the Stonewall Brigade after Thomas Jonathan 'Stonewall' Jackson's death. The bottom line in the incident is that 'Early was late'. Andrew McReynolds' son Frank served in the regiment as Lieutenant and Quartermaster. He was in Ford's theatre on the night that President Lincoln was assassinated and apparently for years to come, it was his 'party piece' to retell the events of that evening. After the Civil War he served on Grand Rapids Police and Fire Commissioners' Boards, and was involved with the creation of the 'Bex Bissell' carpet sweeper company.

General McReynolds went back to that which he loved – practising law – and was District Attorney for Michigan during Andrew Johnson's Presidency.

McReynolds claimed some firsts in his life, such as being in Liverpool when the first locomotive started out with a train, as well as being the first passenger on the first railroad train in the United States. He was also in Baltimore when the first telegraphic message was sent over the wire.[4]

Andrew McReynolds was married to Elizabeth Morgan Brewster, who was seventh in line from William Brewster, one of the Mayflower Pilgrims. In 1862 Andrew's daughter Mary married Frederick Augustine Nims of Muskegon, who was second Lieutenant in the First New York Cavalry. When she died he married her sister Ellen Sloane McReynolds. Frederick was the grandfather of the renowned American poet and academic, John Frederick Nims.

It was in the Nims house that Andrew McReynolds passed away, in November 1898, at the venerable age of 90. There is a McReynolds Avenue in Grand Rapids named in his honour. McReynolds is buried in Fulton Street Cemetery in Grand Rapids, Michigan as is his wife, mother, son, daughter-in-law and grandson.

# Endnotes

1. 'The McReynolds Family', Kerr Family Chronicles, www.dankat.com/kerr/chap6.htm, date accessed 8 May 2013
2. McGee Thomas D'Arcy, 'A History of the Irish Settlers in North America from the Earliest Period to the Census of 1950', Chapter XXIII, 1852, www.libraryireland.com/IrishSettlers/Contents.php, date accessed 13 May 2013
3. Turtle Bunburry, 'The San Patricios and the Mexican War of 1847', http://www.turtlebunbury.com/history/history_irish/history_irish_sanpatricios1847.htm, date accessed 8 May 2013
4. 'Gen.Andrew T.McReynolds', http://kent.migenweb.net/bowen/lp/mcreynoldsAT.htmlBarb Jones, date accessed 24 April 2013

# CHAPTER 9

## Captain Jack Crawford
*The Poet Scout, 1847–1917*

John Wallace Crawford was an Ulster-Scot born in Carndonagh, East Donegal on 4 March 1847. His parents were both natives of Scotland but had moved to Donegal in the Province of Ulster. The father, John Austin Crawford was born in Greenock, Renfrewshire, in 1816 and apprenticed at a young age to a tailor near Glasgow. He was noted for making political speeches and was an advocate of a free form of government. He became such a thorn in the side of authority that he was banished from Scotland with 'a price on his head'. A fishing smack took him the relatively short journey to Co Donegal and there he married the daughter of another 'refugee', Susan Wallace, who was not only a Scot, but claimed descent from no less a personage than Sir William 'Braveheart' Wallace. Indeed in later life Jack Crawford attempted to capitalise on that connection. But Donegal was not to be the final refuge of such an energetic and ambitious family.

In 1861 the Crawford children sailed from Londonderry to join their parents who had emigrated before them to Minersville, Pennsylvania. However, by the time they reached their new home their father had already left, in the company of other Schuylkill County men, to fight in the Civil War. John Austin Crawford spent three months as a Ringgold Volunteer before re-enlisting with Company K of the 48th Pennsylvania Volunteers.

Immediately after his arrival in Pennsylvania young John, though merely a boy, started to work in the coalmines, picking slag for about $1.75 per week. At 15 he lied about his age and joined the Pennsylvania Regulars. His father was wounded twice, initially at Rappamattock and then more severely at the momentous Battle of the Wilderness, which took place from 5–7 May 1864. The following week young John was wounded, aged just 17, at the equally fiercely fought Battle of Spotsylvania. His father died shortly afterwards of a combination of both his terrible wounds and the debilitating effects of alcoholism.

'Jack', as friends now called the young man, was wounded on two more occasions during the Civil War. However, it was his hospitalisation and recuperation during that 'first blooding' that had a significant impact on his life. He was nursed back to health in the Sisters of Mercy hospital near Philadelphia, where the nuns not only cared for him but also taught him how to read and write. Eventually these skills would lead him to a career in writing, but in the short term it allowed him to secure a position as a postmaster in Numidia, Pennsylvania, directly after the War. In September 1869 Jack married the local schoolteacher, Anna Marie Stokes and together they had five children including a girl, who they named May Cody Crawford for Jack's friend William 'Buffalo Bill' Cody.[1]

Jack had written about his Civil War experiences, including a poem entitled, *A Mountain Boy's Letter to General Grant*. However, his poems were never narrowly jingoistic. Indeed one of his poems, *Our First Reunion and Campfire* eerily describes a situation similar to what occurred much later in the Great War in Europe:

> *And often when we shouted*
> *Across to Johnny Reb,*
> *To throw us some tobacco,*
> *And we would throw them bread,*
> *How quickly they responded!*
> *And the plugs came thick and fast*
> *And we shared them with each other–*
> *And shared them to the last.*

Although himself a brave and wounded Union soldier, Jack was never dismissive of Confederate bravery. Indeed he once staged a benefit performance that raised $800 for the ten orphan children of Confederate General John Hood and his wife. He wrote a poem especially for the occasion, entitled *Hood's Children*, in which he celebrated "the brave fighting men of the Blue and the Gray".

In 1875 Jack was appointed as a Captain of the Black Hills Rangers of Dakota. It was at that time that a kinsman of the writer's, Robert McReynolds made Crawford's acquaintance. In his memoir, *Thirty Years on the Frontier*, McReynolds tells us:

> *Captain Jack Crawford, the poet scout, is one of those noble characters*

*whose memory will live so long as records exist of the pioneers who braved the vicissitudes of the frontier and made possible our Western civilization of today. A man of broad mind, daring and brave and yet with all the sweet tenderness of a child of nature, he became great by achievements alone. Others have gained a temporary fame by dime novel writers. Captain Jack, in comparison with others, stands out as a diamond of the first water. He has helped to make more trails than any scout unless it was Kit Carson. That was before the war. During that struggle he was wounded three times in the service of his country. When the war closed he was for many years chief of scouts under General Custer. He laid out Leedville in the Black Hills in 1876, and was of great service to the government in the settlement of the Indian troubles which succeeded the Custer massacre.*[2]

McReynolds commented that although Jack's life was lived in turbulent contexts he was nonetheless someone "who maintained a strictly moral character". He tells us, "I knew him in the 'Hills' in 1876 and have known him ever since, and have always found him to be the same genial, whole souled, brave Captain Jack".[2]

It was at that time, in July 1876, that Buffalo Bill Cody also met Jack for the first time. Crawford replaced Cody as Chief of scouts of the Fifth Cavalry. Cody tells us that that was, "only two months after the Custer massacre at the Little Big Horn, and a mere three weeks after the murder of Wild Bill Hickok in Deadwood". Jack captured both of these events in verse. Indeed some of the revisionists of today suggest that he was one of the creators of what has become known as 'the Custer myth', as here in the poem *The Death of Custer*:

> *I served with him in the army,*
> *In the darkest days of the war:*
> *And I reckon ye know his record,*
> *For he was our guiding star;*
> *And the boys who gathered round him*
> *To charge in the early morn,*
> *War just like the brave who perished*
> *With him on the Little Horn.*[3]

Similarly he was disposed to follow the route of hero-portrayal in his image of Hickok as he pictured his funereal arrangements in the poem, *The Burial of Wild Bill*:

*You buried him 'neath the old pine tree,*
*In that little world of ours,*
*His trusty rifle by his side–*
*His grave all strewn with flowers;*
*His manly form in sweet repose,*
*That lovely silken hair–*
*I tell you, pard, it was a sight,*
*That face so white and fair!*[1]

After becoming Chief Scout for the Fifth Cavalry, under the command of Eugene A Carr, Crawford made a famous horseback ride with urgent dispatches from the Battle of Slim Buttes to Fort Laramie, a distance of 350 miles in four days. This battle took place on the 9 and 10 September 1876 and was the first victory that the US army had over the Sioux after the Little Big Horn. There is an excellent thumb-nail sketch that has come down to us of Jack Crawford's appearance at that time,

"Dressed in buckskin shirt and pants, with a revolver and bowie knife at his waist, and a rifle resting on his shoulder, he is sporting shoulder-length hair and a trim mustache [sic] and goatee."[1]

In 1876 Jack Crawford became an entertainer in Buffalo Bill's Wild West Show. However, their partnership ended in Virginia City, Nevada in the summer of 1877 when, during a combat scene, Crawford accidentally shot himself in the groin. Jack, who was a lifelong teetotaller (a promise that he had made to his mother on her deathbed), somehow blamed the incident on Cody's drunkenness.

The Poet Scout's first book was published in San Francisco in 1879. It contained one poem, called *My Birthday*, written by Jack on his 32nd birthday in which he records, for all his extrovert appearance and bravado, a basic loneliness resulting from a life that separated him so much from family and friends. As he sat in a cabin in Cariboo in distant British Columbia, in sub zero temperatures, where he had been prospecting for gold, he scribbled these lines:

*Lonely in my cabin musing,*
*How the time does pass away–*
*Not a soul to wish me gladness,*
*Not a friend to pull my ears;*
*While my heart is filled with sadness,*
*Thinking of the passing years.*[1]

It is thus not surprising that in the same year of 1879 Jack relocated his long-suffering family from Pennsylvania to the New Mexico territory and began scouting for the army again, this time in their war against the Apache nation. In 1881, whilst out prospecting in New Mexico, five Apache Indians attacked Jack and his two companions and a bullet struck the breech of Jack's rifle. Later examination showed that other bullets had pierced his coat in two places. It had been a 'close shave'.

He also became a post-trader at Fort Craig New Mexico and engaged in ranching and mining. It may be that this 'business' role was what caused Jack's biographer, Darlis A Miller to write, "Jack soon learned that the white man's perfidy could be as deadly to his plans as an Apache ambush."[1]

Ten years later he acted as a Special Agent for the Justice Department, investigating the illegal liquor trade in the Indian Reservations of the Western States and Territories. He continued for the rest of his life to travel the length and breadth of America as an actor, lecturer, special government agent and adventurer, and always paying careful attention to any silver or gold strikes.

Jack Crawford's written accounts of life on the frontier are noted for their true representation of the real dangers that pioneer life entailed. Sometimes Native Americans were portrayed as violent demons and sometimes the description was sympathetic and understanding of the universal human motivations that Jack ascribes to the tribesmen.

In late July 1894 Jack sailed on the steamship *Teutonic* to visit the British Isles starting with a visit to his boyhood home in Carndonagh, where he staged an 'entertainment'. Later he wrote about the visit as follows, "It did my heart good to receive such a reception as that granted me by my townspeople". Standing in the house where he had been born he recalled, "the sunny smile- the sad sweet smile of his mother". Jack also performed to an audience of a thousand people in nearby Londonderry. Amongst those in attendance was the Lord Bishop of Derry and Raphoe, William Alexander, husband of the famous hymn writer who compared Crawford favourably with the American author and poet Bret Harte. The latter's tales of California pioneer life would have been familiar to many in the audience, since Harte had been living in London for almost a decade by 1894.[1]

In later life Jack, who seemed out of place with his family, separated from them and moved back East. He settled in Woolhaven, Long Island, New York, where he died of Brights Disease on 27 February 1917.

### In the Hielans O' Nevada to the Sons of Caledonia[4]

*Awa' ye brawny sons o' Scotland,*
*Up the banks an' doon the braes,*
*Through the Hielans o' Nevada,*
*Sing your sangs o' ither days.*
*This is no sich Cowrie's valley,*
*Nor the Forth's fair sunny side,*
*Nor the grand auld rugged mountain.*
*Farther o' the classic Clyde.*

*Yet just for a while imagine*
*Ye are back on Scotia's shore;*
*'Mang the grouse on hill or heather,*
*Whaur the Hielan' waters roar.*
*Or perhaps in glens o' brecken*
*Whaur the Doon and Afton rin,*
*Thinkin o' your Robby's courtship,*
*By the licht o' bonnie minn.*

*Noble, brave, unselfish poet,*
*Dinna slicht him 'mid your joys;*
*Fill an' drink tae him a bumper–*
*He was Nature's bard, my boys.*
*First o' Scotland's famous freemen,*
*Spurnin' Lords and Monarch's crown;*
*Far ower honest tae be schemin'–*
*Bobby Burns; boys, drink her down.*

*Ride ance mair wi Tam O'Shanter*
*'Till the wutches arch your hair;*
*Smile at Hornbrook's vaunted weesdom,*
*Sigh at Holy Willie's prayer.*
*Prie the he'rty, sonsie Haggis*
*Ere ye rise tae gang awa'–*
*Let the Louse an' Mouse thegither*
*Teach us lessons big an' braw.*

*Up in Heaven wi Hielan' Mary*
*Burns noo sings a sweeter sang,*
*Bootless wearin' brichter laurels*

*Than the men wha did him wrang.*
*"Scots wha hae" methinks I hear it–*
*Hoo sic sparks o'genius shine–*
*At your picnic drain this bumper,*
*"Bobby Burns an' Auld Lang Syne".*

## Endnotes

1. Darlis A Miller, *Captain Jack Crawford, Buckskin Poet, Scout & Showman*, University of New Mexico Press, Albuquerque, 1993
2. Robert McReynolds, *Thirty Years on the Frontier*, El Paso Publishing Co, Colorado Springs, 1906, republished General Books, 2009.
3. Captain Jack Crawford, *The Poet Scout: A Book of Song and Story*, Funk & Wagnalls, New York, 1886
4. Captain Jack Crawford, *Whar' the Hand o' God is Seen and other Poems*, Lyceum Publishing Co, New York, 1910

# CHAPTER 10

## General Sinclair Mulholland

Sinclair Mulholland was born in Lisburn on 1 April 1839. His maternal grandfather, a Captain George Sinclaire, was of Scottish Planter stock. He was a Protestant member of the Third Buffs, 84th Regiment, in which he was active in opposing the 1798 Rebellion. He had married a Catholic, however, and was accused of being something of a 'double agent'.[1]

The name Mulholland is an old Irish name, which is prevalent around the shores of Lough Neagh. The family also had the tradition of being keepers or retainers of the Holy Bells used in ancient liturgy. In Ulster, this Mulholland family were related to some of the Province's most prominent families, including in the family tree the Pottingers, Pollocks, Mays and Dobbs. Sinclair's grandparents are buried in Lisburn's old Kilrush graveyard. Their names were Hugh Mulholland, who was born around the year 1760 and his wife Elizabeth Richardson, who was born around 1773. Hugh died in 1833 some 15 years after Elizabeth had passed away. Hugh and Elizabeth had 10 children, the eldest of which was Henry, who was born in 1796 and it was he who converted to Catholicism. He was Sinclair's father. His first wife was Ann Turtle, who was Protestant, although the children were raised as Catholics.[2] His second wife was Captain Sinclaire's daughter Georgina who had converted from Anglicanism to Presbyterianism and then to Catholicism. Henry at that time was living at The Quay, Lisburn and was a sawyer, coal merchant, timber merchant and 'lighter owner'. His home beside the Lagan at The Quay was at the bottom of Bridge Street and had a small dry dock for repairing lighters, two or three at a time. He also had responsibility for maintaining the lock machinery and for operating the lock at that point on the Lagan Canal.[3]

In 1850, Henry, Georgina and family decided to immigrate to New

York. Not all the family from the first marriage accompanied them. We know that Sinclair's half brother, Joseph Richardson Turtle Mulholland, was an important member of staff with William Barbour Ltd and travelled internationally on their behalf to venues such as America, Belgium and France.[2]

The 1850 census of New York, taken shortly after their arrival, shows the family living in Washington Township, Burlington County and Henry is listed as working as a sawyer once again. It is believed that Henry died about 1856.

In the American Civil War Sinclair distinguished himself and was quickly promoted to Colonel before 1864. He had already received the Medal of Honour by that stage for his outstanding display of courage at the Battle of Chancellorville. He was further promoted through the ranks to reach Major General.[4]

After the war Sinclair moved to Philadelphia and there became Chief of Police. He continued to paint landscapes and write, including a history of his unit, the 116th Pennsylvania, which was part of 'the Irish Brigade'.[4]

In the period 1882–1885, Sinclair lived in Paris and often visited his many friends in Lisburn during that time. When Sinclair died in February 1910, *The Lisburn Standard* carried his full obituary as it appeared in the *Philadelphia Public Ledger*. There is much interest still today in General Sinclair Mulholland amongst American Civil War enthusiasts.[2]

# Endnotes

1. 'Sinclaires-Mulhollands (Belfast and Lisburn)', Sinclair Geneology website, www.sinclairgenealogy.info/sinclaires-mulhollands-belfast-and-lisburn, date accessed 25 April 2013
2. 'General St. Clair Augustine Mulholland M.O.H. 116th Regt. Irish Brigade', The 69th Pa. Volunteer Infantry website, www.69thpa.co.uk/page33.html, date accessed 25 April 2013
3. *These Hallowed Grounds Vol 1: A Record of the Memorials in Kilrush and Saint Patrick's Burying Grounds, Lisburn*, Lisburn Branch of the North of Ireland Family History Society, 2001
4. 'St. Clair Augustine Mulholland', New Advent website, www.newadvent.org/cathen/10626b.htm, date accessed 25 April 2013

# CHAPTER 11

## Alexander Peter Stewart

*Tennessee's highest ranking Confederate Officer*

Readers of my first book, *Legacy: The Scots Irish in America,* may recall Alexander Turney Stewart, a wealthy merchant who was born in Lisburn County Antrim and later, amongst other accomplishments, built Garden City, New York.

However, Turney Stewart had a contemporary namesake who was also Scotch-Irish. His name was Alexander Peter Stewart and the similarity ends with their name and Scotch-Irish heritage. It might be argued that the geography of America was a key reason for the difference, for AP Stewart was born south of the Mason Dixon line.

AP Stewart's parents were William Stewart and Elizabeth Decherd and for the first couple of years of their marriage (1816–1818) they settled in Blountville, Tennessee. Thereafter they lived in the Scotch-Irish town of Rogersville, Tennessee, where Alexander was born on 2 October 1821. Joseph Rogers, who was born in 1716 near Cookstown, County Tyrone, had built Rogersville in 1775. The Stewart family later moved to Winchester, Tennessee and it was there that AP Stewart went to school, before being sent, in 1838, to be educated at the United States Military Academy at West Point.[1]

Alexander Stewart graduated from the Academy in 1842 – it was a famous year for the production of Union and Confederate officers. One classmate was William Tecumseh Sherman and Stewart would later meet him in very different circumstances to that of the college campus.[1] Alexander Stewart served for just one year as an active soldier in the field before being sent back to West Point as a teacher of mathematics. After teaching there for two years in the military, he resigned from the army and accepted a civilian role as Professor of Mental and Moral Philosophy at Cumberland University. Later he moved to the University of Nashville and it was there that he was

ILLUSTRATIONS – SECTION ONE

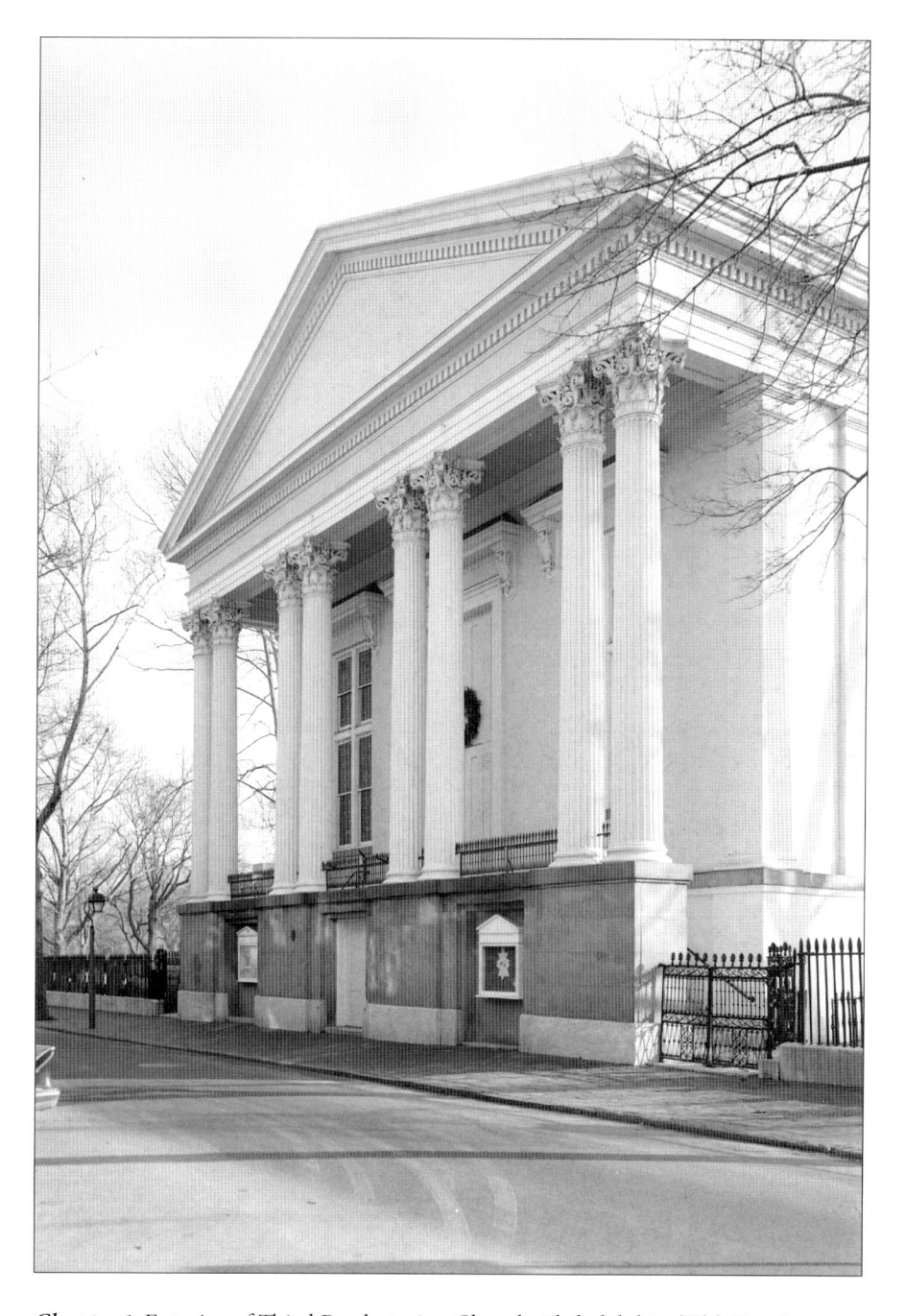

***Chapter 1:*** Exterior of Third Presbyterian Church, Philadelphia, 'Old Pine Street Church', where Rev George Duffield preached.

*Library of Congress, Prints & Photographs Division.*
*Reproduction Number HABS PA,51-PHILA,203--1*

*Chapter 1:* Interior of Third Presbyterian Church, Philadelphia, where John Adams heard Rev George Duffield advocate for Independence.

*Library of Congress, Prints & Photographs Division.*
*Reproduction Number HABS PA,51-PHILA,203--4*

ILLUSTRATIONS – SECTION ONE

*Chapter 2:* Robert Adrain (1775-1843), c1830. Professor of Mathematics at the University of Pennsylvania, and Vice-Provost 1828-1834.

*University of Pennsylvania Archives*

*Chapter 2:* Samuel Brown Wylie (1773-1852), University of Pennsylvania Professor of Ancient Languages 1828-1845 and Vice-Provost 1834-1845, in a painting from 1847.

*University of Pennsylvania Archives*

ILLUSTRATIONS – SECTION ONE

*Chapter 2:* John Fries Frazer (1812-1872), University of Pennsylvania professor of Natural Philosophy and Chemistry and Vice-Provost from 1855 until 1868.

*Public Domain*

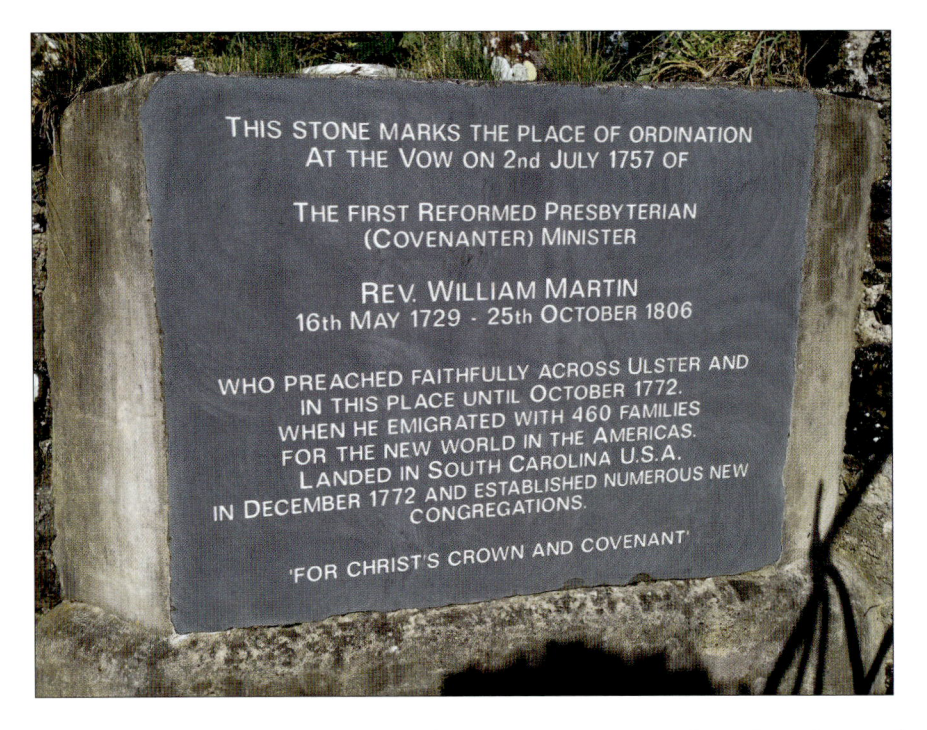

*Chapter 3:* Commemorative stone at The Vow, Co Antrim, marking the ordination and also the American ministry of Rev William Martin.

*Author*

ILLUSTRATIONS – SECTION ONE

*Chapter 4:* James Logan (1674-1751), autographed portrait engraving (c1740).
*University of Pennsylvania Archives*

*Chapter 4:* Logan grave with reference to James Logan in Moira Presbyterian Churchyard, Moira, Co Down.
*Author*

*Chapter 4:* Stenton, the residence of James Logan at Courtland and 18th Streets in Philadelphia, Pennsylvania.

*Library of Congress, Prints & Photographs Division.*
*Reproduction Number HABS PA,51-PHILA,8--2*

ILLUSTRATIONS – SECTION ONE

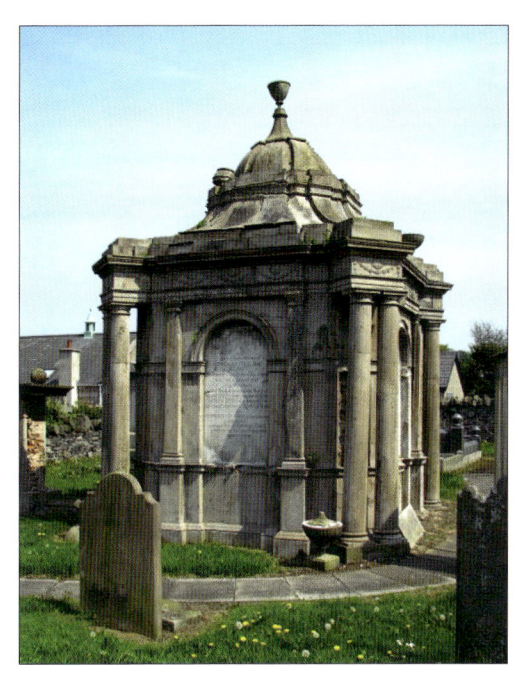

*Chapter 5:* Mausoleum of Thomas Greg (1720-1796), Knockbreda Cemetery, Belfast.

*Copyright Ross. This work is licensed under the Creative Commons Attribution-Share Alike 2.0 Generic Licence.*

*Chapter 5:* Mausoleum of Waddell Cunningham (1729-1797), Knockbreda Cemetery, Belfast.

*Copyright Ross. This work is licensed under the Creative Commons Attribution-Share Alike 2.0 Generic Licence.*

*Chapter 6:* James McHenry, third United States Secretary of War.

*Public Domain*

ILLUSTRATIONS – SECTION ONE

*Chapter 6:* Aerial view of Fort McHenry National Monument and Historic Shrine, at Whetstone Point, Baltimore taken in July 1954.

*Library of Congress, Prints & Photographs Division.*
*Reproduction Number HABS MD,4-BALT,5--3*

*Chapter 7*: John Coffee Hays.
*Library of Congress, Prints & Photographs Division. Reproduction Number LC-USZ62-83948*

*Chapter 8:* Colonel AT McReynolds, First New York Cavalry, c1860.

*Library of Congress Prints and Photographs Division.*
*Reproduction Number LC-DIG-cwpb-06697*

*Chapter 8:* Recruitment poster for the Lincoln Cavalry, otherwise referred to as First New York Cavalry, commanded by Col Andrew T McReynolds, in 1861.

*Library of Congress Rare Book and Special Collections Division,*
*The Alfred Whital Stern Collection of Lincolniana. Portfolio 11, No21*

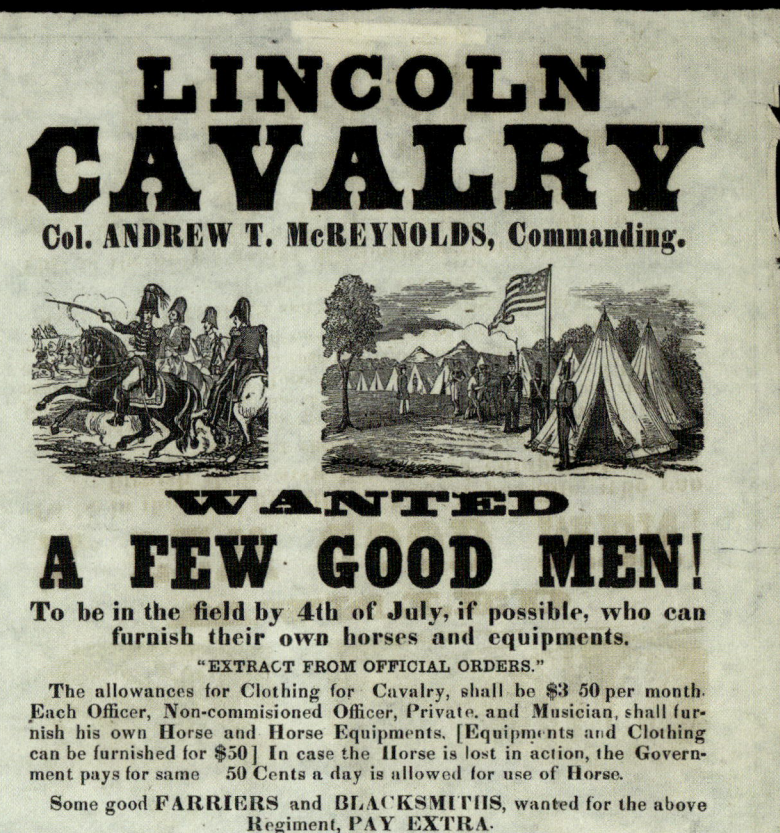

*Chapter 9:* Captain Jack Crawford photographed around 1881.

*Public Domain*

*Chapter 10:* Maj Gen Sinclair Augustin Mulholland.
*Library of Congress Prints and Photographs Division.*
*Reproduction Number LC-USZ62-61455*

employed at the outbreak of the Civil War.[2]

It was then that Stewart entered the Confederate army with a rank of Major of artillery. He would, in time, rise to the rank of Lieutenant General, which was the topmost rank, save one, in the service and the highest-ranking Confederate officer in the Civil War to hail from Tennessee. His soldiers knew Stewart affectionately as 'Old Straight' because of the rectitude of his temperament and stature.

Early in the war, Stewart saw action at Columbus, Kentucky and at the Battle of Belmont. At Shiloh he led his men in repeated desperate attempts in the field, at what was known as the 'Hornet's Nest' and distinguished himself at Chickamauga.[2] As a commander in the field he was quiet and dignified and inspired his men with personal acts of daring bravery, including having horses shot from under him and being wounded by gunshot (albeit superficially). Eventually he surrendered to his former classmate, William T Sherman, in North Carolina.

After the Civil War, AP Stewart was paroled and returned to academia, initially at Cumberland University in Lebanon, Tennessee. In 1874, he was appointed as President of the University of Mississippi ('ole Miss') in Oxford, where he remained for 12 years. When it was decided that the battlefield of Chickamauga should be constituted as a National Park, AP Stewart was installed as a member of the Commission of Planners.

Alexander Peter Stewart died in Biloxi, Mississippi, in 1908. He was one of the last of the old legendary Confederate officers and was considered by his neighbours to be a modest gentleman who pursued literary interests.[2]

# Endnotes

1. 'Tennessee's Highest-Ranking Confederate Officer', Tennessee online, Tennessee's Online History Magazine website, www.tennesseehistory.com/class/APstewart.htm, date accessed 25 April 2013

2. *Dictionary of American Biography*, Vol 18, Steward–Trowbridge, New York, Charles Scribner's Sons, 1946, Public Library of New York, East 42nd Street, NYC, accessed 27 September 2010

# CHAPTER 12

## Samuel Sloan

Samuel Sloan was born on 25 December 1817 in Lisburn. He was the second child born to William and Elizabeth Simpson Sloan (originally spelled Sloane), as a sister, May, had died aged just two weeks old. His father was born in Lisburn in 1794 and married Elizabeth Simpson in Dunmurry, County Antrim in 1815. When Sam was just an infant the family immigrated to the United States. Actually, they landed initially in Quebec as their ship was wrecked in the Gulf of St Lawrence in 1821, where the family lost most of their household goods and stock.[1]

Undaunted the family made their way to New York, where William got a job as a clerk in a linen store owned by John Suffern, an Ulsterman of Huguenot extraction from Nutts Corner. The town of Suffern in Rockland County, New York was founded by him and originally named 'New Antrim'. William obtained employment amongst Ulster friends in New York for most of the rest of his life. When he died, he was employed in the house of Mr William Cowley, trading in 'Bristol and Irish goods'. Cowley, admittedly, was born in Water Street, New York in 1770, although his father St Ledger Cowley had been born in Ireland in 1735.[1]

At 14 years old, Sam was forced to withdraw from Columbia College Preparatory School and found employment as a junior clerk in an importing house on Cedar Street in New York. He remained there for 25 years and eventually became head of the firm having established a reputation for promptness and honesty.

On 8 April 1844, Sam married Margaret Elmendorf and the couple made their first home in Brooklyn. He was chosen as Supervisor of Kings County and President of Long Island College Hospital in 1852. In 1857 he retired from the importing business and was elected to New York State Senate as a Democrat in 1857 but only remained in that position for two years.[2]

Sam Sloan was not to make his illustrious name in importing, however, despite moderate success throughout his career. For the 40 years that followed he engaged in the highly lucrative business of transportation. Wartime is often an unexpected booster of economic needs and that proved to be the case with anthracite, which was needed in greater quantities for the production of arms and armaments during the Civil War. During the nine years when Sam Sloan was President of the Hudson Railroad, which included most of the Civil War years of 1861–1865, the company's shares increased in value by eightfold. Sloan then transferred in 1864 to the Delaware, Lackawanna and Western Railroad and again rose rapidly to become President in 1867. He remained with that company for over three decades.

During the reconstruction years after the Civil War, Sloan expanded into the north and west towards Buffalo and by that time had extended into general freight handling. He spent $1,250,000 on upgrading all his trains to run on anthracite. In the period 1881–1890 coal shipments increased by 32%, general freight by 160% and passenger traffic rose by 88%.[2]

Sloan came to be associated with some powerful figures of the time, including JP Morgan and Commodore Vanderbilt. Gustavus Myers, in *History of the Great American Fortunes,* described Sam Sloan as one of "the monarchs of the land … the actual rulers of the United States, the men who had the power in the final say of what should be done."[3] Hoboken, New Jersey proudly displays a statue of Sam Sloan near its railway station and Wall Street, New York, displays a plaque bearing his name. The town of Sloan in Erie County, New York State was named for him, as was a new locomotive on the Syracuse and Burlington railroad named 'Sam Sloan'.[2]

When he was 80, Sam Sloan visited Lisburn. He was pleased to visit the Presbyterian Meeting House and, as the *New York Times* of 6 March 1898 recorded, "enjoyed the satisfaction of inspecting the baptismal font at which his sponsors had presented him nearly four score years before."[4] As a lifelong Presbyterian, Sam Sloan had put a stop to the running of the railways on Sundays. He explained, "I would not work myself on a Sunday, and I do not see why the men under me should be made to work."

Sam Sloan died in 1907 aged 90 and was buried at St Philip's Church, Garrison, New York. His home, Lisburne Grange still stands at 61 Lisburne Lane, New York, on the Hudson River, with sweeping views of West Point Military College. It was last sold in 2010 for $3,744,325.

# Endnotes

1. 'Sam Sloan's Home Page', http://www.anusha.com/pafg89.htm, date accessed 12 June 2013
2. Richard Palmer, 'A Biographical Sketch of Sam Sloan', The Crooked Lake Review website, www.crookedlakereview.com/articles/136_167/147apr2008/147palmer.html, date accessed 25 April 2013
3. Gustavus Myers, *A History of the Great American Fortunes*, 1909, first modern library edition, 1936.
4. *New York Times*, 6 March 1898.

# CHAPTER 13

## Joseph Seamon Cotter Senior and Junior

Joseph Seamon Cotter Senior was a distinguished black playwright, poet, author and educator, and the father of poet-playwright, Joseph Seamon Cotter Junior. He was born in 1861 on a farm near Bardstown in Nelson County, Kentucky, where his father was a prominent Scotch-Irish citizen named Michael Cotter. The farm belonged to Joseph's maternal great-grandfather, Daniel Stapp, a tanner, who had bought his own freedom and that of his relatives. Cotter's mother, Martha Vaughn, had given her son the name Joseph perhaps because she believed he would be a storyteller, as she herself had been all her life. Prior to Joseph Cotter's birth, his mother had been the personal servant of prominent Bardstown citizen, Rebecca Rowen, wife of Judge Rowen, at the nearby estate of Fairhill. Just two years before she was taken on in this position, another Scotch-Irishman, Stephen Foster, who was a frequent visitor to the home of his cousins, the Rowens, wrote the song *My Old Kentucky Home*. This later became the state song, as it still is today. Martha Vaughn was one of the first people to hear the song being sung in public.

Although he was born near Bardstown, Joseph Seamon Cotter was brought up in Louisville, Kentucky, to which his mother moved when he was just four months old. He learned how to read at just three years of age and was largely self-educated, having left school in 1869 at the end of the third grade in order to help his mother with an income for their home. As a boy he picked rags and later he worked as a teamster in a distillery, a tobacco stemmer, a brick hand and a prize fighter. He learned boxing skills due to his size, as being small he found himself picked on by fellow workers. He also won favour with these tough fellow workers through his skills as a storyteller. When Cotter was aged 22, a prominent Louisville educator called William T

Peyton was impressed by Cotter's ability to write poems. He encouraged the young man, in whom he saw so much promise, to return to education. Cotter took this advice and in 1883 attended Louisville's first black night-school for two five month courses, thereby earning his High School Diploma and Teacher's Diploma. He taught at Cloverdale School just outside Louisville from 1885 until 1887 and at a local private school from 1887 until 1889. He then entered the Louisville public school system at Western Colored School before becoming Principal of the Paul Dunbar School, which was named for the famous black poet who had visited Cotter in 1894 and became a close friend. Cotter then became Principal of the Samuel Coleridge Taylor School[1] from 1911 until 1942 when he retired. He had become a member of the Louisville Board of Education earlier in 1938.

Joseph Cotter married a fellow teacher, Maria F Cox, on 22 July 1891 and they had three children: Leonidas (died 1900), Olivia (died 1914) and his namesake, writer son Joseph Seamon Cotter (who died of tuberculosis in 1919). Cotter senior took an active role in the business and social life of Louisville. He was Director of Louisville Colored Orphan's Society and belonged to the Negro Educational Association, the Storytellers League and the Authors' League of America.

He was a poet of different moods and styles and was the first published poet to deal openly with racial themes. His published books, amongst others, include: *A Rhyming* (1895); *Links of Friendship* (1899); *A White Song and a Black* (1909); *Negro Tales* (1912); and *Collected Poems* (1938). His play *Caleb, the Degenerate: A Study of the Types, Customs, and Needs of the American Negro* (1901) was only the second play by a black American to be published.

Cotter's words, "Learn thou the worth of a dollar and how to keep it from damning thee" are words that come down to all of us in 2013 with great relevance. He died on 14 March 1949.

His son Joseph preceded his father in death by 30 years. In his short life he was a poet, journalist and forerunner of the African American cultural renaissance that took place during the 1920s. He has been described as "the closest thing to an American Wilfred Owen." Joseph Seamon Cotter junior was born in Louisville and although he died at just 24 years of age, he established himself as an innovative voice in the post First World War American poetry scene. He enrolled in Fisk University but had to return home in his second year due to the onset of tuberculosis. On his return home he obtained a position as Editor of *The Leader,* a Louisville newspaper. During this time, grief regarding the untimely death of his sister caused him to write a poem, entitled *To Florence,* which has moved many readers. In

1920 he wrote a one-act play about the First World War, called *On the Fields of France*.

Throughout his work, as with his father's writing, his voice could be angry but despite this, his underlying philosophy was one of hope, as exemplified here in the final verse from his poem *Rain Music*:

> *Slender, silvery drumsticks*
> *Beat the long tattoo—*
> *God, the Great Musician,*
> *Calling life anew.*[2]

Similarly, the words which best describe his struggle and that of his father, "pushing an uphill load", in the America of yesteryear, speak of hope and achievement, "train your head and hands to do, your head and heart to dare."

## Endnotes

1. The school was named after the black English composer (1875–1912) rather than the Romantic poet Samuel Taylor Coleridge (1772–1834).
2. Joseph S Cotter Jr, 'Rain Music', Ed James Weddon Johnson, *The Book of American Poetry*, 1922

## Reference

'Joseph S Cotter Jr', Louisiana Free Library website, http://www.lfpl.org/western/htms/cotter.htm, date accessed 8 May 2013

# CHAPTER 14

## Scotch-Irish settlers in Southern Wisconsin

The main source of background material for this book, about the fascinating and yet conventional chain migration of this community of Scotch-Irish pioneers from Ulster to America, was Anna Dickie, herself an integral member of the Scotch-Irish group. Anna Adams Dickie was born in 1876 in the townland of Ballymacombs, outside the County Londonderry town of Bellaghy. She came to Wisconsin in 1892, which was very much towards the end of the emigration saga for her family and friends. Later Anna was to graduate from Whitewater State Normal School and become a schoolteacher. She died in 1964 and was buried in Oak Hill Cemetery in Sauk County, Wisconsin.

The story which Anna told began back in 1837, with two settlers from the Bellaghy area, namely Roley Godfrey and William Galloway, who immigrated to America in that year. They made their way to Chicago in 1840 and from there to Milwaukee, Wisconsin. In this city they asked locals about where might be a good place to settle and were told about the town of Whitewater in Rock County, in the southern section of Wisconsin. It was to there that they made their way. They encouraged friends and neighbours back home in County Londonderry to join them and in the neighbouring towns of Lima, also in Rock County, and in Koshkonong, in neighbouring Dane County. Notable amongst those who came was John MacMillin, who arrived in 1847.

In America all the friends and neighbours joined with the Presbyterian Church, in spite of the fact that they had not all been members back in Ulster. Although the majority of the Ulster emigrants had been members of Bellaghy Presbyterian Church, erected in 1836 and which still stands, it is known that at least some of the numerous Godfreys who came had belonged to Ballyscullion Parish Church in Bellaghy (and thus were Church of Ireland or 'Episcopalian', as Americans term it), where there are four Godfrey families in the graveyard. In America, the Scotch-Irish immigrants joined with the Presbytery of Chicago, which was allied to the Covenanter branch of the Presbyterian Church. It almost seems that they perceived membership of the Presbyterian Church as being the 'cement' that held their little Bellaghy-based community together in this new land in Wisconsin. They soon elected elders from amongst their ever-increasing number, the first of which were John MacMillin, Francis Vance and Thomas Godfrey. For a time they worshipped in local schoolhouses before they agreed to build a church. Anna Dickie, who refers to her great-uncle as 'Uncle MacMillin', says that he wanted the church to be built on his land but a preferable site was offered by William Alexander, a neighbouring Scotsman. In the tale of this particular migratory settlement there are numerous instances of specific friendship and sharing between this Scotch-Irish Bellaghy group and the nearby communities of Scots who had come directly to Wisconsin from Scotland. The church to which the Bellaghy settlers gravitated was that just north of Lima, about six miles to the west of Whitewater, Wisconsin. In time it grew sufficiently and as is sometimes the case with Presbyterian churches, it split and gave birth to a 'breakaway' at Koshkonong.

The Presbyterians of North Lima initially worshipped in the traditional way, with a precentor using a tuning fork to pitch the tunes for unaccompanied Psalm singing. As happened in Ulster and elsewhere in the 'Presbyterian World', there was much upset in the North Lima church when hymns and organ playing were introduced to the worship format. Some Presbyterian groups in the 'Celtic fringe' areas, such as the Hebridean islands off the west coast of Scotland, still worship in the traditional way today.

Anna Dickie's account presents the reader with a fascinating portrait of some of the families who settled in this area of south Wisconsin close to the Illinois border.

Anna Dickie's great-uncle, John MacMillin, having rationalised and maximised the family farm at Bellaghy, and been elected as an elder in Bellaghy Presbyterian Church at 25 years of age, eventually joined the rest of the family in the spring of 1847. With him came neighbour John Armstrong's family. After a six week voyage they made their way via the Great Lakes to Milwaukee, Wisconsin, which lies on the western side of Lake Michigan.

The journey took a heavy toll on the group, with a high number of fatalities occurring, including John's sister Nancy, who died along with her baby during childbirth. John described her as a strong woman, "she could shear her rig with any man and then dance on the green at eventide." Anna Dickie tells us, almost 'matter of fact', that "such afflictions were common on the frontier." Amidst the suffering and hardship of their migration it seems not just impossible but somehow incongruent that the group carried with them such a luxury as fine bone china wrapped carefully in Sphagnum moss.

During that first autumn ('fall') season in Wisconsin, John and William captured, enclosed and fed some hogs, which were running around wild. They butchered the fattened pigs before carting them off for sale in Milwaukee. The hogs' hair, which was removed during butchery, was mixed with clay that first winter and the resulting concoction used on the cabin walls as a temporary substitute for more expensive lime plaster.

With so much land available compared with the situation around Bellaghy the families bought up all they could. They became 'land-rich', with the Godfreys owning more land than the other settlers, despite the Kyles being the most numerous clan. However, this land investment stretched their finances to their limit.

William and Mary Kyle were originally married in Castledawson Presbyterian Church. The community began to open out a little from Bellaghy, in terms of place of origin, although they emanated from the same region of Ulster. From nearby County Antrim came Boyds, McWhineys, Kyles, Harrises, McCartneys, Barcleys, Glasses, other Kyles and McNamees. Loudens and Lees came from the shores of Lough Neagh.

In 1942, Herbert Godfrey composed and read a poem at a homecoming at North Lima Presbyterian Church. In it he pictured his ancestors and their struggles in the New World.

> *When immigrants from other lands –*
> *Our forbears, Christian folks –*
> *Came way out West and settled here*
> *Among Wisconsin oaks.*

## Reference

Anna Adams Dickie, 'Scotch-Irish Presbyterian settlers in Southern Wisconsin', *Wisconsin Magazine of History*, Vol 31, No 3 (1947–1948), available at http://content.wisconsinhistory.org/cdm/ref/collection/wmh/id/17038, date accessed 13 May 2013

# CHAPTER 15

## Old Ripy Whiskey

*Distilled by an Ulster family in the 'Tyrone' distillery Kentucky*

Over the centuries, a number of families had settled in Scotland and temporarily adopted the country as a safe haven from either racial or religious persecution in their homeland. One such family were the Ripy clan (spelled Rippey in eighteenth century Ulster). They were Huguenot and the progenitor of the County Tyrone branch was Dr William Ripy, who had fled his native France to Scotland shortly after the St Bartholomew's Day massacre of Huguenot Protestants in 1572. Eventually William Ripy relocated to County Tyrone as part of the settlement of West Ulster in 1610.[1]

One branch of the family was established at Ballymagorry, which is some four miles north of Strabane on the Derry Road and where much of the Plantation settlement was organised by Sir George Hamilton of Greenlaw (died 1654), brother of James Hamilton who became the first Earl of Abercorn. It is believed that Dr Ripy and the Earl of Abercorn were firm friends and went hunting together. That Dr Ripy was a person of some refinement is evidenced by the fact that he brought a fine mahogany wine set with him as a treasured possession.

The history of the family in Ulster may be gleaned from references to their affairs in various census records and in the Abercorn Papers. Thus in the Hearthmoney Rolls of 1666, there is a reference to 'Hugh & Betty Reppy (sic) Scavagherin'. *The Survey And Valuation Of The Manor Of Cloghogle 1777 (Abercorn Papers) Ballymagorry,* lists Matthew Rippey as a tenant living at Milltown. The list a decade later shows him still living in what is now listed as Upper Milltown. A letter from the Earl's agent Henry Pomeroy to His Lordship on 30 August 1778 mentions Nathan Rippey of Drumclamph as being a first cousin of another Abercorn tenant, namely Abraham Boys. The Flaxgrowers' Census of 1796 mentions 'Rippey, Nathan Ardstraw Tyrone' as having, "one wheel" and 'Rippey, William Ardstraw Tyrone' having "four wheels". Three members of the Rippey family received the 1796 Irish Flax Growers subsidy, namely, William, Nathan and Matthew.[2]

William Rippey married twice. His first wife was Elizabeth Lyons and they had five children, John, William, Hugh, Robert and Elizabeth. John's son James (1811–1872) immigrated to Philadelphia in 1832 and from there moved to Kentucky, where he settled in Lawrenceburg. At first he engaged in the dry goods business, before changing to the wholesale liquor business and in 1869 he established the distillery that was later operated by his son, Thomas B Ripy (1847–1902). The brand was named 'Old Ripy' and the distillery itself 'Tyrone', and thus the village that grew around it in Anderson County, Kentucky took the same name. In 1888, the Southern Railway built Young's High Bridge over the Kentucky River at Tyrone.[1]

In 1893, 'Old Ripy' was chosen from a list of 400 bourbons to represent Kentucky at the World Fair in Chicago. Ernest Ripy, who was then the family member in charge, retired and subsequently his son reactivated the brand somewhat when Prohibition ended in the United States. The Ripy family were involved in various distilleries including 'Old Hickory Springs', which changed its name in 1935 and reopened as 'Ripy Bros Distillery'. In 1940, 'Wild Turkey Whiskey' was started by Thomas McCarthy and was designated as 'Wild Turkey NYC'. It was owned by the firm of Austin, Nichols & Co. Wild Turkey Whiskey was not specific to any one distillery but by 1971, Ripy Bros was the only distillery they were using. In that year Austin, Nichols & Co purchased Ripy Bros outright and labelled some whiskey as 'Wild Turkey' and some as, 'Old Ripy' but the Old Ripy distiller Jimmy Russell distilled both.

'Wild Turkey' was the name settled on and it became the best-selling bourbon in the USA. In 1980, all was sold to the French firm of Pernod Ricard. In turn, in April 2009, the Italian group Campari bought the bourbon brand from Pernod Ricard for a sum of $575 million.

It had been a long journey from France to Scotland to north Tyrone in Ulster but the Ripy family had brought something of each of these locations to the product that they distilled in Tyrone, Kentucky, and which became a world-renowned success.

We know that the family did not disappear entirely from Ulster as Joseph, who was also one of John Ripy's sons, born in 1859, returned to live there and the Ulster Covenant signatures of 1912 show that one Matthew Rippey of Castlegore signed the document.[1]

# Endnotes

1. 'The Rippeys', McAskies of Ardstraw, www.mccaskie.org.uk/Rippeys.htm, date accessed 26 April 2013
2. 'Ballymagorn, Leckpatrick Parish Rentals and Valuations, 1666–1858', Official County Tyrone website, extracts from Abercorn Papers, PRONI, and Family History Centre, Derry, http://freepages.genealogy.rootsweb.ancestry.com/~cotyroneireland/rental/ballymagorry.html, date accessed 8 May 2013

# CHAPTER 16

## Thomas Wolfe

Thomas Clayton Wolfe was born on 3 October 1900 in Asheville, North Carolina, the youngest of eight children born to William Oliver Wolfe and Julia Elizabeth (nee Westall). It was through his mother's maternal relatives, the Penlands and the Pattons, that he inherited his Scotch-Irish roots. Both of these families settled in western North Carolina long before the Revolutionary War. Wolfe's great-great-great-grandfather, George Patton, was married to his own full cousin Nancy Patton. The cousins were the offspring of two Scotch-Irish brothers, Robert and Aaron Patton. Indeed George Patton's sister Elizabeth was the second wife of the iconic Scotch-Irish frontiersman and politician, David Crockett.[1]

Thomas Wolfe is widely recognised as one of the most revered American novelists of the early twentieth century. So much so that William Faulkner, who was Scotch-Irish himself, said that Wolfe was "his generation's best writer", and then Faulkner modestly (or perhaps not so modestly) listed himself as second in that ranking. Wolfe is reckoned to have been a major influence on beat generation writer Jack Kerouac, who wrote *On the Road* and also the modern day author Philip Roth.

Wolfe's mother was a formidable businesswoman and invested in a focused way in real estate. In 1906, she bought a boarding house at 48 Spruce Street in Asheville, which was nostalgically named 'Old Kentucky Home', notwithstanding that it stood in a town in North Carolina. She moved into this house with young Thomas whilst the rest of the family continued to live nearby at 92 Woodfin Street in Asheville. 'Old Kentucky Home' was designated a Natural Historic Landmark in 1971.

Thomas' father was a successful stone-carver who ran a gravestone engraving business but was much given to periodic bouts of drunkenness, during which he would typically bombard his family with torrents of general verbal abuse, interspersed with lengthy renditions of passages from the works of William Shakespeare. Wolfe was later to portray both his father and his mother with great vigour and in a satirically humorous vein.[2]

Shortly before he was 16, Thomas Wolfe entered the University of North Carolina at Chapel Hill. There he wrote for the school magazine and became editor of the College newspaper, *The Tar Heel*. Having graduated at 20, Wolfe continued his university education at Harvard, where he studied playwriting. He was later, in 1935, to 'savage' what he perceived as the pretentious atmosphere of Harvard in those years in *Of Time and the River*. Initially he was attracted to the notion of a career in writing for the theatre but had continual difficulty in getting his plays produced. He took a job as an English Lecturer at New York University in 1924 and worked there on an on/off basis for the following six years.

In 1925, he travelled to Europe and on coming home in August of that year he met Alice Bernstein, a set and costume designer, who was married and also almost 20 years his senior. They began a tempestuous love affair which lasted for five years.

In 1938, Thomas Wolfe developed a form of tuberculosis of the brain and died in John Hopkins University in Baltimore, Maryland. He was then interred with his parents, William Oliver and Julia, in Riverside Cemetery, Asheville. He left behind a huge reservoir of unpublished writing. A great deal of the material was published posthumously and that process continued into the 1980s. President Bill Clinton listed the posthumously published *You Can't Go Home Again* (1940) as one of his 'Top 21' novels and this autobiographical work is often seen as Thomas Wolfe's masterpiece.[3]

More recently, *Return of An Angel* by Sandra Mason is a play which portrays Wolfe's family, their reaction and that of the citizens of Asheville to the publication in 1929 of his novel *Look Homeward Angel*. Each year on 3 October it is performed in a theatre immediately adjacent to the Thomas Wolfe Memorial, in celebration of Wolfe's birthday. Fittingly, a collection of his work is held by his *alma mater,* the University of North Carolina at Chapel Hill.[4]

Thomas Wolfe's work portrayed, with powerful impact, the America that existed before the Second World War and did so with a pyrotechnic vocabulary that stunned his readers with its uniqueness.

# Endnotes

1. 'Penland Spotlight', Penland Historical Society website, http://penlandhsinc.homestead.com/PenlandSpotlight.html, date accessed 24 June 2013
2. David Herbert Donald, *Look Homeward: A Life of Thomas Wolfe*, Harvard University Press, 2003
3. 'Bill Clinton's 21 Favourite Books', CBS news website, http://www.cbsnews.com/2100-250_162-585068.html, date accessed 24 June 2013
4. The Thomas Wolfe Society website, http://www.thomaswolfe.org/, date accessed 24 June 2013

# CHAPTER 17

## John Steinbeck

*and his maternal Ulster-Scots family – the Hamiltons of Ballykelly*

Samuel Hamilton of Mulkeeragh, Ballykelly was the maternal grandfather of the Nobel Prize-winning novelist John Steinbeck. Although Steinbeck was just two years old when his grandfather died, he had a lifelong fascination with Samuel and as the years went by sought to find out more about the Hamiltons and his own roots in Ulster.[1]

Samuel Hamilton was baptised in Ballykelly Presbyterian Church on 7 October 1830 and immigrated to America when he was aged 17, at the height of the Potato Famine. He followed thousands of others from the island of Ireland who sought refuge from the ravages of the Great Hunger. Samuel Hamilton made his way initially to New York, where he married a girl from home called Elizabeth Fagan. Shortly after this the couple found themselves in the initial vanguard of those people who headed out for California, where the Hamiltons settled on and built up a ranch near King City, which is about 60 miles from the city of Salinas at one end of the valley which bears the same name.[2]

Ballykelly and Mulkeeragh lie within the Limavady estate which was purchased and settled by Ulster-Scots in 1698. William Conolly, MP for Londonderry County and later Speaker of the Irish House of Commons, purchased the land and over a number of years brought in what James I had termed 'British' settlers or planters. The Hamiltons were amongst the earliest families in this particular phase of settlement. In papers available in the Public Records Office, Titanic Quarter, Belfast, reference is made to Ulster-Scots from this area that were part of the 1718 exodus to New England, which was really the initial wave of Ulster-Scots immigration to America. Amongst their number was one John Hamilton 'of Mulkeeragh'. From this phrase, 'of

Mulkeeragh', it is possible to surmise that in 1718 the Hamiltons had been at that location for some time.[2]

Samuel Hamilton's own parents lived in the vicinity. His father, also named John, married Esther Clarke and made his home there. Steinbeck's great novel, *East of Eden,* was published in 1952 and began its life as a factual chronicle of his family's history in both Ballykelly and California. At some critical point this work was morphed into a fictional format. Although the format was changed, the Hamilton name was not altered. Within this new context the Hamiltons, particularly Samuel, were drawn 'true to life'. As regards the journey out to California, the repetition and rhythm of this and similar odysseys represented for Steinbeck a fundamental truth; that this "moving and westering" provided the dynamic which actually built America. This may explain why the Hamilton ranch was at the heart of Steinbeck's writing. It is the setting for his classic story for young people, *The Red Pony* and was the work space in which the young John Steinbeck learned many of the practical skills that he retained all his life.[3] Steinbeck's biographer, Jay Parini, tells us that, "Like his grandfather Hamilton, he was a practical man who liked to work with his hands: to fix things, carve wood, build a boat, hang a door."[4]

In *East of Eden,* Steinbeck informs the reader that,

> *"young Samuel Hamilton came from the north of Ireland and so did his wife. He was the son of small farmers neither rich nor poor, who had lived on one landhold and in one stone house for many hundreds of years."*

Steinbeck comes close to suggesting that the Hamiltons of Mulkeeragh might well have been 'cousins' of Sir James Hamilton, as were many of the Hamiltons of the time who settled on former church lands, such as those at Mulkeeragh. He hints at this possibility in the novel,

> *"Hamiltons managed to be remarkably well-educated and well read; and, as is so often true in that green country, they were connected and related to very great people and very small people, so that one cousin might be a baronet and another cousin a beggar."*[5]

One of the most potent and enduring 'direct' references to the Ulster homeland occurs in a passage in *East of Eden,* where Samuel Hamilton 'remembers' attending a public hanging during his boyhood in Ballykelly's neighbouring city of Londonderry,

> "He saw himself, a very little boy, so small that he had to reach high for his father's hand. He felt the cobbles of Londonderry under his feet and the crush and gaiety of the one big city he had seen."

The imagery of the ironic side-show, the claustrophobia and the need to be protected by his father from seeing the full horror of the 'spectacle' suggests an anecdote passed down in family folklore.[5]

Samuel Hamilton's wife, John Steinbeck's grandmother, is portrayed unfavourably in the novel and some of her negative traits are attributed to her Ulster roots,

> "she had a dour Presbyterian mind and a code of morals that pinned down and beat the brains out of nearly everything that was pleasant to do."

Liza was also described as having,

> "...a finely developed sense of sin. Idleness was a sin, and card playing, which was a kind of idleness to her. She was suspicious of fun whether it involved dancing or singing or even laughter."[5]

In that same year of 1952, when *East of Eden* was first published, Steinbeck made the first of two journeys to Ballykelly in a vain search for his Ulster home. He described this fruitless search in *Colliers Magazine*,

> "we were looking for a place called Mulkeeragh. You can spell it half a dozen ways and it isn't on any map. I knew from half-memory that it was near to Ballykelly, which is near to Limavady, and I knew that from Mulkeeragh you could look across the Lough to the hills of Donegal."[1]

Steinbeck never found the remnants of the house, however, the late Annesley Malley, an expert surveyor, guided me to the site from the Foyleside area. The Steinbeck description is entirely accurate looking "across the Lough to the hills of Donegal", etc.

The graveyard of Ballykelly Anglican church contains gravestones which record Hamiltons having passed away in 1870, 1875, 1876, 1916, 1942, 1944 and finally, in 1950, John Steinbeck's great-aunt Mary E Hamilton, who was known to be a staunch unionist and the last in the line of that particular branch of the family. Just across the road, in the graveyard of the Presbyterian Church which the family attended, lie the remains of Elizabeth Hamilton Ritchie who passed away in 1948. Steinbeck was really just a couple of years too late in his visit to meet living Hamilton kinsfolk. Steinbeck felt that his journey was none the less valuable. He described Ballykelly in this way, "the seat of my culture and the origin of my being and the soil of my background." These evocative words encapsulate the feelings that many Americans hold in the matter of their Scotch-Irish roots.

I have trawled through *East of Eden* and extracted many other direct and indirect references to the Hamiltons and comments on their typicality in terms of their ethnic background. If you have not read the novel for some time (I had not read it since my teens), go back and read it with a fresh perspective in mind. To do so is very valuable.

## Endnotes

1. Ed Pascal Covici JR., *The Portable Steinbeck*, Viking Portable Library, Revised 1976 Edition. It contains an essay originally published in *Collier's Weekly* entitled 'I go back to Ireland', 31 January 1953.
2. Hearthmoney Rolls, PRONI HMR 1663 John Hamilton, Straw, Boveragh maybe the common ancestor of the Roe Valley Hamiltons.
3. Ed Jackson J Benson and Susan Shillinglaw, *America and Americans, Selected Fiction and Non-Fiction by John Steinbeck*, Penguin Classics, 2003
4. Jay Parini, *John Steinbeck: A Biography*, Henry Holt, 1996
5. *East of Eden*, Viking Press, 1952, Penguin Kindle Edition 2000

# CHAPTER 18

## Clayton McMichen and Jimmie Rodgers

The name McMichen is derived from the Scots-Gaelic 'Mian', as a shortened version of Michael. Other names with the same root are, McMahon, McMeekin and McIlveen. Clayton McMichen's Scotch-Irish ancestors came to the North Georgia area in the early 1800s and settled near Altoona, where they worked as farmers.[1]

It was there that Clayton was born on 26 January 1900. As an 11 year old schoolboy he learned to play fiddle with his uncles and his father. The latter was in fact a trained musician and taught the boy tunes such as *Durang's Hornpipe* and *The Arkansas Traveller*. When Clayton, nicknamed initially 'Mac' and then much later in life 'Pappy', was 13 years of age the family moved to Atlanta, Georgia and the lad commenced an apprenticeship as a motor mechanic.[2]

However, it is for playing the fiddle that he is today remembered, and not just for playing, but for being a virtuoso and innovative performer. No greater accolade could be granted to him than these words of the late Bill Monroe, the 'father' of Bluegrass, "back in the early days he was the best". Although Clayton was exceptionally adept at 'old-style' fiddle playing, he was also one of the first to develop the jazzy 'swing' fiddle idiom. He formed his first band in 1918, as a teenager and initially it was dubbed 'Lick the Skillet'. Later this was changed around to 'The Skillet Lickers'. McMichen's broadcasting career began in 1922 on Radio Station WSB. In the early 1920s, the Georgia railroad system operated an on board train 'radio' service that was 'in-house' and operated solely for its own passengers. It was there that McMichen broadcast many of his 'tunes' such as *Lonesome Mama* and *Dixie*. McMichen's first solo success occurred in 1927 with a number entitled *Sweet Bunch of Roses*, which sold in excess of 100,000 records.

The Skillet Lickers broke up in 1931 and McMichen formed a new band called 'The Georgia Wildcats'. The band included Thomas Hoyt 'Slim' Bryant, who passed away relatively recently, on 28 May 2010, aged 101 years old,[3] as well as the late Carl Cotner and Merle Travis from Muhlenberg County, Kentucky.[1] Cotner and Travis much later, in 1982, recorded an album with Mac Wiseman entitled *The Clayton McMichen Story*.

As McMichen's playing evolved, it developed as a fusion of country, folk, jazz, swing and pop into one of the most distinctive fiddle styles and sounds. Some have even labelled him 'the fiddler of the century'.

In 1932, McMichen began a very productive period of playing with Jimmie Rodgers. The latter is often listed as also being of Scotch-Irish origin and along with the Carter family is sometimes credited as being the originator of Country Music. Jimmie Rodgers, the 'Singing Brakeman' was born on 8 September 1892 in Meridian, Mississippi, the son of a railway foreman. In his career in music Jimmie Rodgers sold 12 million records. His career began when he recorded *Blue Yodel (T for Texas)*, which went to Number One in the Music Charts of 1928. His style included blues, yodelling and European folk music. Although Rodgers passed away in 1933, in 1961 the Country Music Hall of Fame was initiated and his was the name of the first inductee to be registered, albeit posthumously. In 1997, Bob Dylan enlisted the help of a galaxy of stars including Bono, Van Morrison and Aaron Neville to record the album *The Songs of Jimmie Rodgers, A Tribute*.[4]

Sixty five years earlier, in 1932, Jimmie Rodgers had written to Clayton McMichen and offered him some session work. When 'Mac' offered to come and bring 'Slim' Bryant with him, Jimmie wrote back as follows, "Mr Peer says he wonts (sic) me to do at least 10 numbers so if you have anything be sure to bring it along."[1] They met in August of that year in Washington DC and travelled to a session in Camden, New Jersey. During the sessions Rodgers became ill and McMichen had to administer morphine shots to him in order to kill the pain. Notwithstanding this acute situation, they collaborated on a McMichen song which 'Mac' had already recorded called *Prohibition Blues* and also on the classic *When it's Peach Picking Time Down in Georgia*.

When speaking about McMichen's 1937 version of 'The Georgia Wildcats', which included 'Slim' Bryant, Riley Puckett, Merle Travis and Lester Flatt, Pee Wee King once said, "They were the Glenn Miller of the Country Music field".

For the rest of his life Clayton McMichen worked and lived in Louisville, Kentucky, where he felt somewhat in the shadow of emerging stars such as Bob Wills, who of course was playing out of Texas with his band 'The Texas

Playboys'. In retrospect, some today consider that McMichen was the finer musician of the two but it may be that Kentucky was not the centre of the creative musical activity that he needed at that time. 'Pappy' McMichen worked for a time as a used car salesman and owned and ran a bar at 300 Spring Street, Louisville, Kentucky. Occasionally McMichen came out of 'hibernation' and there were glimpses of the old brilliance, as in 1964 at The Newport Folk Festival and in 1968, when 'Pappy', then as old as the century itself, was placed first in the senior division of the 'Kentucky State Fiddling Championship'.[1]

On a very personal level, the very titles of his tracks evoke in me a sense of Scotch-Irish life in the Appalachians, with numbers such as *McMichen's Reel, Paddy Won't You Drink Some Cider, Give the Fiddler a Dram, Rickett's Hornpipe, Shortening Bread* and *Singing an Old Hymn* all echoing back up along the river valleys to the Ulster homeland.

Also evocative of everyday life amongst the 'Mountain Folk' are titles that he recorded such as *Blue Ridge Mountains of Virginia, In the Hills of Old Virginia, Smoky Mountain Home, My Blue Ridge Mountain Queen* and the unforgettable *When it's Peach Picking Time Down in Georgia.*

# Endnotes

1. 'Clayton McMichen Biography', Bluegrass Messengers website, http://www.bluegrassmessengers.com/clayton-mcmichen-biography.aspx, date accessed 26 April 2013
2. *The New Georgia Encyclopaedia*, www.georgiaencyclopedia.org, date accessed 26 April 2013
3. Tony Russell, 'Slim Bryant Obituary', *The Guardian*, 27 July 2010, http://www.guardian.co.uk/music/2010/jul/27/slim-bryant-obituary, date accessed 26 April 2013
4. Tony Russell, *Country Music Originals: The Legends and the Lost*, Oxford University Press, 2010

# CHAPTER 19

## Moon Mullican

*Co-Writer of 'Jambalaya' and King of the Hillbilly Piano Players*

Aubrey Wilson 'Moon' Mullican was born on 29 March 1909 into a Scotch-Irish farming family in Corrigan, Polk County, Texas. The Mullicans were a deeply religious family who farmed 87 acres with some sharecropper help right on the Texas/Louisiana border. Indeed that Cajun proximity was to have a big effect on Moon's musical composing and playing.

The name Mullican and its family of names – Milligan, Milliken, Mulligan, etc – originated in County Donegal. Aubrey's branch had gone to Scotland from there but his ancestor James Mullikin had 'returned' to Ulster and lived for a period before settling originally in Maryland in the mid 1600s. It is not known precisely where James lived in Ulster but Sir William Petty's Census of Ireland in 1659 suggests that most of the 'returned' Scottish Mullicans had settled in South Antrim.[1]

Moon's family had moved from Maryland to the southern states and he was born the son of Oscar and Virginia Mullican on a farm that was surrounded by substantial forest and logging communities, who enjoyed a rambunctious musical style of boogie woogie piano playing and gut bucket country blues guitar picking. His grandfather Private Wilson G Mullican, who was born in Tennessee, had served with the Sixth Mississippi Infantry Regiment CSA, which was organised in 1861. Comprised of 649 men, 76% of which were lost at the Battle of Shiloh, it surrendered in 1865 with just 60 men left.

Aubrey's musical career began when Oscar spent $20 on purchasing a new pump organ, which he thought would be useful for encouraging the boy and his sisters to learn tunes that could accompany hymn singing. However, around the same time, eight year old Aubrey had made friends with Joe Jones, one of the black sharecroppers on the farm, who introduced him to country blues. The result was tension at home with his strict father. Local legend has it that 14 year old Aubrey played piano in a café in Lufkin, Texas, which lies to the north of Corrigan and that the boy walked out of one session with $40 in tips bulging out of his pockets. East Texas musicians then could and did listen to a variety of music including Cajun, New Orleans and Chicago jazz, gospel, blues, hillbilly and pop.[2]

Aubrey was influenced by all of this and left home aged 16 for Houston, where he began playing and singing in clubs. He employed a style of piano-playing which he described as one, "to make the beer bottles dance" on top of the piano.

By the 1930s Aubrey had earned the nickname 'Moon' and evolved a style that was much influenced by Bessie Smith, 'Blind' Lemon Jefferson and Leroy Carr, and in the Country idiom, Jimmie Rodgers and Bob Wills. He also played with and recorded with Cliff Bruner's 'Texas Wanderers' at that time. Early in the 1940s Moon recorded *Truck Driver's Blues* and *I'll Keep on Loving You* with that outfit and had settled by then into a pattern of writing his own songs and 'covering' African American blues of the time.

By 1945, Moon had his own band called 'The Showboys' and in 1947 he wrote the classic *New Jole Blon*. At that time he would typically play a country song followed immediately by a saxophone-driven blues. During the later 1940s, he had great influence on then emerging stars such as Jim Reeves, who was a band member for a time, and also on Hank Williams, who described Moon as his "favourite artist". By the end of the 1940s he was inducted as a member of 'The Grand Ole Opry', the highest accolade that can be awarded to musicians working in the, 'Country Music' genre.

Moon was later to influence stars such as Bill Haley, Elvis and of course he was a key influence on Jerry Lee Lewis. He is also credited with co-writing the iconic country Cajun classic *Jambalaya* with fellow Opry star Hank Williams and was not able to get full recognition for doing so because of his contract with King Records. Tellingly, he drew 50% of the royalties on the song for the rest of his life.[2] It is sometimes suggested that it was one of a number of songs that Hank bought from Moon at that time, including the sequel to *Jambalaya*, which was written from the point of view of 'Yvonne', the girl named in the song. It was entitled *I'm Yvonne (Of The Bayou)*. In 1958, Moon was signed up by the famous Owen Bradley at Coral Records and recorded an album entitled *Moon over Mullican*. He is also believed to have jammed on stage with Buddy Holly around that time.

By the 60s his career had begun to fade, although he was still playing locally. In 1962, he suffered a heart attack on stage and although he recovered for a time he died of cardiac arrest on the morning of 1 January 1967 and was survived by his wife Eunice. They did not have any family together. He was buried in Magnolia Cemetery, Beaumont, in Jefferson County, Texas. On his gravestone are inscribed the words "I'll sail my ship alone", which was the name of one of his hits.

Moon Mullican's contribution to the evolution of both country music and rock and roll was immense and sadly little recognised today. Almost single-handedly he developed a form of Honky Tonk Music in which the mother was western swing and the father was a mixture of juke-box and tavern.[3] He was known as the 'King of the Hillbilly Piano Players' and was a major influence on the development of Jerry Lee Lewis'[2] music, which in time provided an interesting piano-based counterpoint to the guitar led Rockabilly sound of another Sun Record prodigy, Elvis Presley.

## Endnotes

1. Sir William Petty's *Census of Ireland*, 1659. Published by Pender, Co Antrim, PRONI 15A/72. Petty was an economist loyal to Cromwell and the Census names those holding land in seventeenth century Ireland. Information is arranged by county, barony, parish and townland.
2. 'Moon Mullican Biography', AllMusic website, http://www.allmusic.com/artist/moon-mullican-mn0000594267, date accessed 24 June 2013
3. Tony Russell, *Country Music Originals: The Legends and the Lost*, Oxford University Press, 2010

# CHAPTER 20

## Elvis Aaron Presley

A couple of years ago I visited Elvis Presley's birthplace in Tupelo, Mississippi and when there noticed a sign which made reference to Elvis' Scotch-Irish ancestry. The plaque bore an inscription as follows:

> *Northern Mississippi was settled by frontier folks from areas including North and South Carolina by way of the Appalachian Trail. Gladys Smith's ancestors included a Scotch-Irishman who married a Cherokee woman.*

The sign was intriguing and called out for further research.

Elvis' great-great-great-grandmother, Morning Dove White (1800–1835), was a full-blooded Cherokee who married William Mansell in 1818 in West Tennessee, where he was a settler. William, who was born about 1795, was the son of Richard Mansell. He had been a soldier in the Revolutionary War and either he, or his father, had emigrated from Ulster. The Mansells were originally Norman French, who had settled in Scotland before coming to Ulster. They later moved on to the American Colonial lands early in the eighteenth century.[1]

William Mansell, aged just nineteen, fought along with Andrew Jackson in the brutal Indian Wars. He fought at the Battle of Horseshoe Bend, Alabama and later in Florida. When the war was over he returned to West Tennessee and headed into its Indian territory to find himself a bride.[1]

The late Elaine Dundy in her acclaimed biography *Elvis and Gladys,* said that through that marriage William gained,

> *"age old Indian knowledge of the American terrain, of forests and parries;*

*of crops and game; of protection against the climate; of medicine lore; healing plants as well as something in which the Indians were expert – the setting of broken bones."*

She added that maybe that was where Elvis got his complexion and clean cheek line.[2]

So William and his new bride headed for Alabama and settled in Marion County in the north west portion of the state near the Mississippi border. At that time the Scotch-Irish were the predominant settlers in the north of Alabama. William Mansell built himself a substantial house there, near what is now the town of Hamilton but was then known as 'Toll Gate'. The town was later renamed after AJ Hamilton who was a Confederate army officer.

William and Morning Dove had three children. During the Civil War, one son, James Jordan Mansell, was a Private in Company A, Spencer's Regiment of the First Alabama Cavalry, which was a Federal Company unit of the Union Army. William was actually a spy for the Union cause. He was captured and executed by one Ruben Capling near the Chickasaw River in Colbert, County Alabama in either the fall of 1864 or the spring of 1865.[1]

William's eldest son, John, was born in 1828. He was Elvis Presley's great-great-grandfather. Elaine Dundy described him as "half Scots-Irish, half Indian, (but) seems to have grown up wholly, 'wild injun'."[2] He had many legitimate and illegitimate children and his descendants are still plentiful in North Alabama and North East Mississippi. He married Elizabeth Gilmore, who may also have been Scotch-Irish, and he squandered the family farm. In 1880, he moved to Oxford, Mississippi and changed his name to Colonel Lee Mansell. His sons moved to Saltillo, Mississippi near Tupelo.

White Mansell, who was Elvis' great-grandfather married Martha Tackett, who was Jewish and a neighbour in Saltillo. It was thus that Elvis gained his Jewish ancestry.

History was not kind to the Mansells. The Mexican War, the Civil War and the financial depression that eventually hit the all important cotton crop, eroded their position until they were forced to sell their lands and become sharecroppers. It was not a totally grim life, however, and the family found solace in religion, music and the simple pleasure of country picnics.

The Mansells had handsome features and Octavia, sometimes called 'Doll', who was Gladys Presley's mother, was a noted beauty in her day. At 27 years of age she married her first cousin Bob Smith. In her young days Elvis' mother Gladys worked in a shirt factory and was said to have somewhat resembled the movie actress, Clara Bow. She also danced a mean 'Charleston' and Elvis was said by some to have inherited good looks and his 'moves' from her.[1]

But what of the Presleys? That plaque, which I mentioned earlier at Elvis' birthplace in Tupelo said that Elvis' father, "Vernon Presley was descended from a Scotch blacksmith who immigrated in 1745. Gladys and Vernon had farmers and sharecroppers in their family trees, and experienced hardship, doing without, and wishing for better within their lifetimes".

There is some disagreement amongst historians about the origin of the Presley name. One source puts suggests the original name was German ('Bressler') and emanated from the Palatinate village of Hochstadt. This version has Valentin Bressler as the founder of the family, who immigrated to New York in 1710.[3] A contrary view has the original American Presley as David Presley from Lonmay, Aberdeenshire, who settled with his son Andrew in New Bern, North Carolina in 1745. Interestingly, some records of this man describe him as an "Anglo-Irishman". We know that Andrew fought Battle of Eutaw Springs in 1781. The battle was fought under the command of Scotch-Irish General, Griffith Rutherford, who lost his eldest son James in the engagement.[4]

Vernon Presley's father, Jessie Dee Presley (1896–1973), was a sharecropper in summer and worked as a lumberjack in winter, drifting from Mississippi to Kentucky and Missouri. He was a 'sharp dresser', handsome and dark. In 1935, Gladys gave birth to twins, Jesse Garon, who was stillborn and Elvis Aaron. The spelling of Aaron was to emphasise the 'A' and thereby enable the close rhyme with Garon.[1]

In religion the family belonged to the First Assembly of God Church, and visitors to the birthplace can now visit the little white church of Elvis' boyhood, which has been moved to the site. Using technology very effectively, they can also partake in a 'virtual' gospel meeting with the hymns and songs of the 'King's' earliest days.

Also significant is the fact that the Presleys lived near a black area of Tupelo, known as the 'Shake Rag'. It is said that Elvis first ventured there with Vernon, who had a job delivering groceries at one stage. Other accounts say Elvis went there often with two black pals of his, namely Sam Bell and Bo McClinton, and that he once met Muddy Waters there. He himself testified that this was important in *The Charlotte Observer*, 26 June 1956:

> I used to hear old Arthur Crudup bang his box the way I do it now, and I said if I ever got to the place I could feel all old Arthur felt, I'd be a music man like nobody ever saw.

Real Elvis fans will know that Elvis' first recording for Sun Records was *That's All Right Mama,* which was an Arthur 'Big Boy' Crudup song. Sun Records is based in Memphis, West Tennessee, to which Elvis' family moved when he was just 13 years old. Living in Memphis in his adolescent years, Elvis had not forgotten the sounds of Tupelo that he had absorbed as an impressionable youngster.[5]

## Endnotes

1. 'Elvis Presley Family History 1669–1935', Elvis Australia website, http://www.elvis.com.au/presley/biography/elvis_presley_family_history.shtml#sthash.4BR9MzBy.fDIcr04i.dpbs, date accessed 24 June 2013
2. Elaine Dundy, *Elvis and Gladys,* Macmillan Publishing Company, New York, 1985
3. 'Elizabeth Bressler/Pressler Family of Niederhochstadt/Pfalz and Berks County Pennsylvania', *Pennsylvania Genealogical Magazine,* XXXVII: 4:341-366, 1992
4. 'Elvis roots lead to Scotland', quoting Scottish author Allan Morrison from Greenock. BBC News website, http://news.bbc.co.uk/1/hi/scotland/3559331.stm, date accessed 26 April 2013
5. 'Elvis Presley Birthplace: 306 Elvis Presley Drive, Tupelo', Leaflet

# CHAPTER 21

## Adlai Stevenson I and II
*Grandfather and grandson*

Back in February 1900, the *Chicago American* newspaper ran a photograph of former Vice President Adlai Stevenson holding his new grandson, who had been baptised with the exact same name, Adlai Ewing Stevenson.

That year the grandfather had been once again nominated to run for Vice President on the Democratic ticket. Half a century later his grandson would run twice as the Democratic nominee for President of the United States and thereby gain even greater national and international prominence.

Vice President Stevenson's parents were John Turner Stevenson and Eliza Ewing Stevenson. John Turner Stevenson's grandfather William had emigrated from Ulster in 1748. It was the family's own belief that their Stevenson antecedents had lived in Belfast. It has been sometimes suggested that it was those Scotch-Irish emigrants who gave the Vice President his strong character and his deeply held religious convictions. In Belfast it is believed that the family worked in the 'hat' industry and were Wesleyan in their religious observance.[1]

The Stevensons landed first in Pennsylvania, before making the archetypal Scotch-Irish journey onwards to North Carolina, down the Great Wagon Road and then to Kentucky, where they arrived and settled in 1813, as both pioneers and minor slaveholders. In 1852, when Adlai was aged 16, a severe frost wiped out the family's tobacco crop for that year. This caused Adlai's father to set free all their few slaves and move to Bloomington, Illinois, where he operated a sawmill.

Young Adlai qualified as a lawyer and in 1860, aged 25, he obtained his first public office as Master in Chancery. This was a post that he held throughout the period of the Civil War. In 1874 and again in 1878, he was elected to serve Illinois in the House of Representatives. He was appointed as

Vice President of the United States, under President Grover Cleveland and held that office from 1893–1897.[2]

Adlai Stevenson was admired for the dignity that he brought to the position. He was particularly commended for his non-partisan treatment of individuals. Physically he posed an image of some gravitas, being six feet tall and, "of fine personal bearing and uniformly courteous to all". In 1896, he was briefly mentioned as a possible successor to President Cleveland but lacked sufficient support to mount a realistic campaign for the top position. His wife Letitia was one of the founders of the Daughters of the American Revolution (DAR), which she viewed as a means of healing the wounds that had opened between the north and south of the country, as a result of the Civil War. Vice President Stevenson died in Bloomington, Illinois on 14 June 1914.[2]

His namesake grandson, Adlai Ewing Stevenson II, grew up well aware of his heritage. He once described it thus,

> *"my father's family moved to Kentucky from Virginia and North Carolina and a generation or so later they moved on to Bloomington, Illinois before the Civil War. They were Scotch-Irish Presbyterians and Democrats, and strong in the faith, both political and religious".*

Adlai II was actually born in Los Angeles on 5 February 1900 but when he was five the family moved back to Bloomington, which had become home for the Stevensons. When he was 12 he met President Woodrow Wilson. During that meeting, President Wilson told the boy that he himself had been President of Princeton University before he began his political career. The visit had a visible effect on the life of the adolescent Adlai Stevenson. Woodrow Wilson became his role model in life. That was so much the case that Adlai set and achieved a personal goal of graduating from Princeton, even though none of his family had previously attended the University.

Adlai Stevenson attended the Unitarian Church in Bloomington, which had been founded by his maternal grandfather, Jesse Fell. When he was resident in the Lake Forest, Illinois, he held membership of the Presbyterian Church, largely because there was no Unitarian worship in that City. He was comfortable with this joint membership.

Adlai Stevenson became Governor of Illinois in 1948 by a huge majority and was twice Democratic candidate for President in 1952 and again in 1956, being defeated by the hugely popular war hero Dwight Eisenhower on both occasions.[3]

On his inauguration in 1961, President Kennedy appointed Adlai

ILLUSTRATIONS – SECTION TWO

*Chapter 11:* Lt Gen AP Stewart, drawn by Alfred R Waud, c1864.
*Library of Congress Prints and Photographs Division.*
*Reproduction Number LC-DIG-ppmsca-20282*

*Chapter 12:* Portrait of Railroad Executive Samuel Sloan c1907.

*Public Domain*

*Chapter 12:* Delaware, Lackawanna and Western Railroad yards, Scranton, Pennsylvania, c1890s.

*Library of Congress Prints and Photographs Division.*
*Reproduction Number LC-D4-11616*

*Chapter 13:* Joseph Seamon Cotter Senior in an image from an 1903 edition of his play *Caleb, the Degenerate*.

*Public Domain*

*Chapter 16:* Portrait of Thomas Wolfe by Carl Van Vechten, 14 April 1937.
*Library of Congress Prints and Photographs Division.
Reproduction Number LC-USZ62-42508*

ILLUSTRATIONS – SECTION TWO

*Chapter 17:* Some of the Hamilton family graves at Ballykelly Presbyterian Church. There are also graves of the family in Tamlaght Finlagan Parish Church nearby.

*Author*

*Chapter 17:* Location of Mulkeeragh, the Hamiltons' former home, Ballykelly.

*Author*

*Chapter 18:* Clayton McMichen.

*Courtesy the Dixie Archive*

ILLUSTRATIONS – SECTION TWO

*Chapter 20:* Inside the house where Elvis was born.

*Author*

*Chapter 20:* Plaque marking the birthplace of Elvis Presley.

*Author*

KITH AND KIN

*Chapter 20:* A typical black sharecropper home in the Mississippi delta near Greenville.

*Author*

*Chapter 20:* Scotch-Irish church and graveyard, Mississippi.

*Painting by Carole McReynolds Davis, kin to the author.*

ILLUSTRATIONS – SECTION TWO

*Chapter 20:* Scotch-Irish cabin, Oktibbeha County, Mississippi.

*Chapter 20:* Old School house where four McRenyolds brothers taught, Oktibbeha County, Mississippi.

*Both paintings by Carole McReynolds Davis, kin to the author.*

*Chapter 21:* Vice President Adlai Ewing Stevenson I, c1892.

*Library of Congress Prints and Photographs Division. Reproduction Number LC-USZ62-44296*

*Chapter 21:* Ambassador Adlai Ewing Stevenson II photographed in June 1961.

*Library of Congress Prints and Photographs Division. Reproduction Number LC-DIG-ppmsca-19603*

ILLUSTRATIONS – SECTION TWO

*Chapter 22:* Dr Wallace Hume Carothers who spearheaded Du Pont's first decade of basic organic chemistry research and developed Nylon.

*Public Domain*

*Chapter 23:* Statue of Gen John Stark, Concord, New Hampshire.

*Library of Congress Prints and Photographs Division.
Reproduction Number LC-D4-36221*

ILLUSTRATIONS – SECTION TWO

*Chapter 23:* A photograph of the grave marker of Matthew Thornton, signer of the United States Declaration of Independence. It is located in the Matthew Thornton Cemetery in Merrimack, New Hampshire.

*Courtesy Magicpiano under the Creative Commons Attribution-ShareAlike 2.5 Generic License*

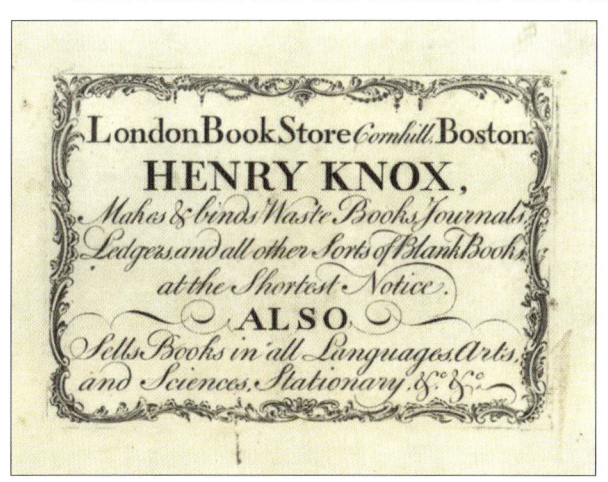

*Chapter 23:* Trade card to the 'London Book Store' in Boston run by Henry Knox.

*Public Domain*

*Chapter 23:* Asa Gray, considered the most important American botanist of the 19th century.

*Public Domain*

ILLUSTRATIONS – SECTION TWO

*Chapter 24:* One of the McLellan family homes in Portland, Maine, showing the wealth the family briefly enjoyed.

*Library of Congress Prints and Photographs Division.*
*Reproduction Number HABS ME,3-PORT,6-1*

*Chapter 24:* Interior parlor with fireplace in a typical McLellan family home, Portland, Maine.

*Library of Congress Prints and Photographs Division.*
*Reproduction Number HABS ME,3-PORT,6-3*

*Chapter 27*: Portrait of Francis Hutcheson by Allan Ramsay, circa 1745. Wearing a black academic gown over a brown coat, Hutcheson holds a copy of Cicero's *De Finibus*.

*Public Domain*

Stevenson as United States Ambassador to the United Nations. It was whilst he was involved in this role and walking in the streets of London, on 14 July 1965, that he collapsed and died. Shortly after this, the United States took the uncommon step of issuing a postage stamp in his honour.[4]

Adlai Stevenson was known for his witty and urbane reflections on life. Eisenhower once famously called him an "egghead". He was passionate about democracy and human rights.[3] This is well encapsulated in his words during a speech in Detroit, Michigan in 1952, when he said, "My definition of a free society is a society where it is safe to be unpopular."[5]

## Endnotes

1. Jean H Baker, *The Stevensons: A Biography of an American Family*, Norton Paperback, 1997
2. 'Adlai Stevenson I', wikipedia website, http://en.wikipedia.org/wiki/Adlai_Stevenson_I, date accessed 24 June 2013
3. 'Adlai Stevenson II', wikipedia website, http://en.wikipedia.org/wiki/Adlai_Stevenson_II, date accessed 24 June 2013
4. Richard Henry, 'The Biography of Adlai Stevenson', in the *Dictionary of Unitarian and Universalist Biography*, an on-line resource of the Unitarian Universalist History & Heritage Society, http://www25.uua.org/uuhs/duub/articles/adlaistevenson.html, date accessed 8 May 2013
5. 'Adlai E Stevenson Jr. Quotes', The Quotations Page website, http://www.quotationspage.com/quotes/Adlai_E._Stevenson_Jr./, date accessed 24 June 2013

# CHAPTER 22

## Wallace Hume Carothers
*Inventor of Nylon*

Wallace Hume Carothers was born in Burlington, Iowa on 27 April 1896 and was the eldest of four children. His paternal ancestors were of Scottish origin, having settled in Pennsylvania before the Revolution. His maternal forebears were Scotch-Irish, however, and were for the most part artisans and farmers. Carothers' mother, Mary Evalina McMullin of Burlington, Iowa, exerted a powerful influence and guidance in his early years. From those Scotch-Irish McMullins, Carothers developed a love of literature and above all a love of music, which remained with him all his life.[1] He was particularly devoted to his musician sister, Isobel, who was famed as 'Lu' of the radio trio 'Clara, Lu and Ern'. When she died in January 1937, it was a devastating blow to Wallace Carothers who, although he had a brilliant mind, was also 'a troubled soul' or perhaps more starkly, a 'manic depressive'.

Wallace Carothers' father, Ira, who was born in Illinois, was a teacher and Vice President of Capital City Commercial College, Des Moines, Iowa. It was there that his eldest son commenced his College Education, initially studying Accountancy rather than the Chemistry for which he was to become world-famous. Subsequently, in September 1915, Wallace entered Tarkio College, Missouri, in order to pursue studies in Science, whilst at the same time teaching accountancy in the same college.[2] With America's entry into the First World War, he was asked to teach Chemistry and after obtaining his BSc in 1920 he enrolled in the Chemistry Department of the University of Illinois. From 1921–1922 Carothers taught Analytical and Physical Chemistry at the University of South Dakota. It was about that time that he embarked on investigation of independent problem-based research projects.

Carothers received his Doctorate in 1924 and at the graduation ceremony the University staff considered him to be "one of the most brilliant students who had ever been awarded the doctor's degree". Carothers stayed on in Illinois for a further two years before moving to join the faculty of the prestigious Harvard University in 1926. His biographer, Roger Adams characterises Carothers during that time as follows:

*He was still the same quiet, methodical worker and scholar, not forceful as a lecturer, but careful and systematic in his contact with students.*[1]

In 1928, he moved to a position with the Du Pont Company, who had planned a new programme of analytical research. Carothers was selected to lead the team of Organic Chemists at its experimental station at Wilmington, Delaware. He was allocated a small group of trained research chemists to work on projects of his own devising. In the nine years that followed, he made fundamental contributions to theoretical science, as well as laying the foundations for the development of new materials that were of significant commercial importance. Carothers and his team were the first to investigate the properties of the acetylene family of chemicals, which eventually led to exploration of acetylene polymers and the development of neoprene. In 1931, this was manufactured as synthetic rubber and is still widely used today in the petrol and oil pipes in motorcars, in garden hoses, insulated wire and work gloves.[3]

However, impressive that neoprene is in itself, Carothers would exceed it by far. His research team began to focus on the development of a synthetic fibre that could be spun strong and could replace silk. Carothers had a theory that certain polymers could be produced by condensation through an elimination of water. Thereby he obtained 'superpolymers' and refined this through a long process involving alternating reactions to acids and alcohols, and heating in a vacuum context.

On 28 February 1935, he developed a resin and numbered the specimen '66' because it contained six carbon atoms. The product came to be called Nylon and was characterised by the number 66. The material was such that it gained considerable strength by drawing the fibre under tension and thus causing a reorientation of the crystals.[4]

Initially, the product was known as 'Tiber 66', until September 1938 when it was first used in toothbrushes. Of course the big break came in 1940, when women's stockings hit the shelves in the stores in the USA. On that first day over 5 million pairs of nylon stockings were sold. Soon nylon was being used in all the various ways that we now take for granted.[4]

Wallace Hume Carothers died too soon to see the impact that his invention would have on industry and modern everyday life. Carothers had argued seriously with his parents over an affair that he had with a married woman and when his beloved sister passed away in January 1937, he was never able to reconcile himself to her loss. This was despite the fact that in February 1936 he married a 'new' love and Du Pont colleague, Helen Everett Sweetman.[2] A daughter, Jane, was born in November 1937 but she never knew her illustrious father, who has so long battled with depression. On 29 April 1937, a couple of days after his forty-first birthday, Carothers took his own life by consuming cyanide. He believed he had not achieved much in his life, ironic considering all that he had accomplished. This inventive genius, the son of fairly ordinary Scottish and Scotch-Irish Americans, had developed a product that was arguably the most revolutionary fibre that had been created in thousands of years.

## Endnotes

1. Roger Adams, 'Memoir of Wallace Hume Carothers', *National Academy of Sciences of the United States of America Biographical Memoirs*, Vol XX, presented to the Academy at the general meeting 1939. Available online: www.nap.edu/html/biomems/wcarothers.pdf, date accessed 26 April 2013
2. Mary Bellis, 'Wallace Carothers – History of Nylon', About.com Inventors website, http://inventors.about.com/od/nstartinventions/a/nylon.htm, date accessed 26 June 2013
3. Ed Matthew E Hermes, *Enough for One Lifetime: Wallace Carothers, Inventor of Nylon*, American Chemical Society and Chemical Heritage Foundation, 1996
4. 'Wallace Hume Carothers', Cal Poly Pomona University website, http://www.csupomona.edu/~nova/scientists/articles/caro.html

## Reference

Eds H Mark and GS Whitby, *Collected Papers of Wallace Hume Carothers on Polymeric Substances*, Interscience Publishers Inc, New York, 1940. Available online: http://archive.org/details/collectedpaperso031072mbp, date accessed 26 June 2013

# CHAPTER 23

## Scotch-Irish settlement in New England

### Rev James McGregor

In 2004, the Presidential hopeful who ran against George W Bush was Senator John Kerry of Massachusetts. On his maternal side, Kerry's sixth great-grandfather was Rev James McGregor.

James McGregor (1677–1729) was the Presbyterian Minister in Aghadowey, County Londonderry, who famously led his congregation and their friends in the 'five ships' exodus from the port of Coleraine to Boston in 1718. They eventually built the Scotch-Irish settlement of Londonderry, New Hampshire together. *The Encyclopaedia of the Irish in America* refers to James McGregor as "the Moses of the Scotch Irish in America".

James McGregor is reputed to have been a full cousin of Scottish folk hero Rob Roy McGregor. When James was but a lad of 12 years old he found himself inside the Siege of Derry. As previously mentioned, young James is reputed to have fired a cannon from the top of St Columb's Cathedral in the city, by way of announcing that a merchant ship, *The Mountjoy*, had broken the boom (or barrier) that had been constructed across the River Foyle to prevent supplies getting through to the starving Protestants within the walls. These Protestants had been besieged by the Jacobite troops of James II for 105 days. Rev Edward Parker in his *History of Londonderry NH*, 1851, commented on this, saying of McGregor's role,

> "Thus habituated to hardship and denial he was well prepared to share with the company who took possession of this spot, the toils, dangers, and sacrifices of ease and comfort, ever attendant upon a new settlement."[1]

When James McGregor was Presbyterian minister of Aghadowey he was nonetheless known as 'the Peacemaker'. His wife Maryanne and he were the parents of ten children and they were poor. However, there were a few wealthy landowners within his congregation, such as his father-in-law, Elder David Cargill and his brothers-in-law, James McKeen and Captain James Gregg. It is believed that they helped finance the voyage. Before departing, McGregor preached a last sermon from a text in Exodus, "If thy presence goes not with me, carry us not up hence."[1]

On 4 August 1718, the brigantine *Robert* arrived in Boston harbour with McGregor and 16 families of his congregation on board. They were given a poor reception by the Bostonians and stigmatised as 'Irish'. McGregor wrote in disgust of this to Governor Shute. He protested at the 'Irish' label, as they were in fact Scots living in Ireland and stated his surprise, "when we so frequently ventured our all, for the British crown and liberties." After taking temporary refuge in Dracut, Massachusetts, McGregor made his way to the spot that was later to be called Londonderry, New Hampshire. There, on 12 April 1719, at Beaver Lake he preached his first sermon in the New World. This time he took as his text Isaiah 32:2 and asked God to provide "a hiding place from the winds and a covert from the tempest, as rivers of water in a dry place; as the shadow of a great rock in a weary land."

As the years passed McGregor added extra assurance to this plea and took 'his gun well loaded and primed' to the pulpit every Sunday, prepared to repel any sudden Indian attacks. However, Londonderry was never attacked by Indians. Some say that this was because they respected the Scotch-Irish for not having stolen their land. Others claim that Indians were afraid to attack due to the reputation of the settlers. Perhaps it was simply that there was no major river running through the town for Indian canoes to paddle through on their journeys. In any case the town had garrison houses in both East Derry and Derry village within its boundary and also a log palisade or 'flankers', which surrounded Rev McGregor's house.

On 21 June 1722, Londonderry received its charter from Governor Shute of Massachusetts and John Wentworth of New Hampshire on behalf of King George I of Great Britain. James McGregor was no longer a poor man. His had been the first 'framed' house built in the town and he had also received three out of the 132.5 shares of Londonderry, plus a bonus of 250 extra acres of land. By 1723, the population of Londonderry had reached 2,400 souls and in the mid eighteenth century Londonderry was the second largest town in New Hampshire.[2]

## Rev Matthew Clark

After Rev James McGregor died, another Reverend who had suffered the Siege of Derry arrived in Londonderry, New Hampshire. He was Rev Matthew Clark of Kilrea and although never formally installed, this 70 year old took to his role of pastor with great vigour and humour. Again, Parker particularly portrays his mischievous sense of fun and use of the Ulster Scots idiom when he was preaching.

Matthew Clark was wounded at the Siege of Derry as a result of "a ball grazing the temple", which affected the bone so that it never healed. The sore that was thus provoked was concealed using a black patch, as may be seen in any contemporaneous portrait of the cleric. His conduct in church, though no doubt serious in purpose, was immersed in a great deal of humour, which was often expressed in his Scotch-Irish tongue. For example:

One Sunday morning, Clark was preaching when a handsome young British officer in his bright red uniform entered the church and stood at the back. Many of the young ladies of the congregation were much excited at the sight of this fine specimen of manhood, and began to snicker and whisper. Clark spoke to the young man, "Ye are a braw lad, ye ha'e a braw suit o' claithes, and we h'ae seen them, ye may sit down." On another occasion his preaching touched on Simon Peter's role at the Garden of Gethsemane and he remarked, "Just like Peter, aye mair forrit than wise, ganging swaggering aboot wi' a sword at his side; an' a puir han' he mad' o' it."

Like David McGregor, Matthew Clark also taught in the local school and in 1729 was paid an 80 pounds annual amount to preach and an additional 40 pounds if he would "save our town from keeping any other grammar school master". Clark was a temperate man and a vegetarian, which was relatively unusual during this period. His third wife was the widow of Rev James McGregor.

When he died on 25 January 1735, in accordance with his special request, his body was carried to the grave by those who had been his fellow-soldiers and fellow-sufferers in the Siege of Derry.[2]

## David McGregor

David McGregor was the son of Rev James McGregor. He was born in County Londonderry in 1710 and travelled with his parents and siblings to New England. In time he would follow his father into the ministry but the first reference that we find to his employment in Londonderry, New Hampshire is in 1725, when he is recorded as the town's first school teacher.

He was later ordained and in 1737, when the pulpit became vacant at the First Parish Church, many citizens felt that David would be the natural successor to this position. After all this had been the church of his father, without whom arguably there would have been no Londonderry, New Hampshire. However, the church elders had different ideas and instead appointed the Rev William Davidson from Scotland. In theological terms Davidson represented new, or perhaps different, thinking. He professed to be something of an Arminian, believing that ultimately salvation came through faith rather than as a Divine gift, which would have been the orthodox Presbyterian view at the time.

The citizens were divided on the matter and those who held David McGregor's beliefs built their own church. Controversially, they levied a tax on each and every resident of the town, regardless of personal view on the matter. The church became known as the West Parish Church and every Sunday some 40 families crossed to the west of the city to worship there. By the same token the same number of families crossed from the west to worship at First Parish Church. Often they met on the sidewalk whilst en-route. David McGregor was to remain pastor of this congregation until his death in 1777. Three years earlier, in 1774, his son James opened a store in the East Derry Hill area of Londonderry.

David McGregor's daughter Margaret married Captain James Rogers, brother of the more famous Major Robert Rogers who founded the corps of tough fighting men who were known as 'Rogers' Rangers'. Much later David McGregor's great-granddaughter, Jane Means Appleton, became the wife of President Franklin Pierce.[2]

## Matthew Thornton

Matthew Thornton was one of three Ulster-born men who signed the Declaration of Independence. He was born in County Londonderry in 1714 and his family emigrated when he was just three years old with the 1718 exodus. The Thornton family settled, not at Wiscasset as is often stated but just outside Brunswick, Maine on a plot of land overlooking Maquoit Bay, on Rossmore Road. In 1976 Brunswick Knights of Columbus placed a granite marker on the site of the former Thornton homestead.

In 1720 Brunswick was at the confluence of three major cultures, each seeking territory. This consisted of the English in Boston and in Falmouth to the west; Native Americans to the north and the interior of the state; and the French of Acadia, Nova Scotia and the St Lawrence to the east. As a Scotch-Irish American, Matthew Thornton's life was touched by all three.

In 1722 he and his family narrowly escaped an Indian attack when their house was burned down. The Thorntons made their exit hurriedly by canoe and first took refuge in the Casco Bay area before settling for a time in Worcester, Massachusetts. It was here that young Matthew received his early education. Eventually he qualified as a Doctor of Medicine, started a practice in Londonderry, New Hampshire and became a wealthy citizen. He joined the part-time militia and rendered good service as its medical officer in the 1745 British expedition against the French, which culminated at Fort Louisburg in Cape Breton. Matthew Thornton married in 1760, aged 46.

By the momentous year of 1775, Londonderry was the second biggest town in New Hampshire. In that year, Matthew Thornton was elected President of the Convention that was taking place to decide on what shape a new independent America might take. In the following year he became President of the Fifth Congress which adopted the First Constitution of the Colonies. He also chaired the five-man committee that produced the 'Constitution' document and after its adoption, he was elected as the First Speaker of the House. In the period 1776–1782 Thornton served as Chief Justice of the Court of Common Pleas and from 1784 until 1787 he was a member of the New Hampshire Senate.

Matthew Thornton died in 1803 aged 89 whilst on a visit to the home of his daughter in Newburyport, Massachusetts. There are many tributes to his memory in the United States, including 'The Matthew Thornton High School' in Londonderry, New Hampshire and a monument placed over his grave in 1887.[2] An amusing image of Matthew Thornton emerges in a letter from John Adams to his wife Abigail, written from Baltimore on 15 February 1777. Within the letter Adams shares with his wife some of the droll wit of Matthew Thornton:

> *We have from New Hampshire a Colonel Thornton, a physician by profession, a man of humor. He has a large budget of droll stories with which he entertains company perpetually. I heard, about twenty or five and twenty years ago, a story of a physician in Londonderry, who accidentally met with one of our New England enthusiasts, called exhorters. The fanatic soon began to examine the Dr concerning the articles of his faith and what he thought of original sin. 'Why', says the Dr, 'I satisfy myself about it in this manner. Either original sin is divisible or indivisible. If it is divisible, every descendant of Adam and Eve must have a part, and the share which falls to each individual at this day is so small a particle that I think it is not worth considering. If indivisible, then the whole quantity must have descended in a right line, and must now be possessed by one person only; and the chances are millions and millions to one that that person is now in Asia or Africa, and that I have nothing to do with it.' I told Thornton the story, and that I suspected him to be the man. He said he was. He belongs to Londonderry.[3]*

## General John Stark

Archibald Stark, the father of John Stark, was born in Glasgow in 1697 and educated at the University of Glasgow. At a young age he moved with his father and family to Londonderry in Ulster, where he married Eleanour Nichols, who was herself the daughter of a Scottish immigrant. In 1720 he headed for New Hampshire, where Rev McGregor and his band of followers had already acted as pathfinders. He was accompanied by a party of adventurers from Ulster and it was a bad difficult voyage, on which his children died. On arrival of the emigrant ship in Boston, in the late autumn of that year, it was clear that there was smallpox on board. So, in a now familiar pattern, the ship travelled up to Maine, where the Starks settled on the Sheepscot River near Wiscasset.

Eventually Archibald Stark, like so many other Scotch-Irish immigrants in New England before him, made his way to Londonderry, New Hampshire. It was here that the future General, John, was born on 28 August 1728. When he was eight years of age the family moved to Derryfield, now known as Manchester, New Hampshire.

In 1745 we find Archibald as a volunteer in a local militia company set up to protect the local people from attack by Indians. His sons, William, John, Samuel and Archibald were all commissioned into the British army. William, who was the eldest, served under General Wolfe at Louisburg and Quebec in French-controlled Canada.

John Stark lived at home with his family until 1752, when in late April of that year he was kidnapped by Abenakis whilst on a hunting trip. He was eventually freed just over two months later and greatly impressed his captors by the way that he protected himself whilst running the gauntlet which was a ritual required by the terms of release. During his time as captive, John Stark gained great insight into the terrain, as well as the hunting and warfare methods of the Native Americans. This was to prove inspirational and beneficial to him for the rest of his life. It was no surprise when the Governor commissioned John Stark as Second Lieutenant in Major Robert Rogers' Rangers. He fought against the forces of French General Baron Dieskau and was wounded and taken prisoner.

John Stark did not return to military service again until 23 April 1775, four days after the Battle of Lexington and Concord, and the outbreak of the Revolutionary War. This time he was fighting against the British, with a rank of Colonel of the New Hampshire Militia. He was subsequently given command of the Third New Hampshire Regiment and marched south to Boston to support the blockaded rebels there. Stark and his forces arrived just as General Howe landed troops and the Battle of Bunker Hill ensued. Drawing on his experience, Stark was able to take a strategic view, read British military minds and 'plugged gaps' in the patriot American defences. He ordered what have been described as 'withering' fusillades of firing, which decimated British redcoat lines, particularly when they charged Stark's 'Minutemen' forces. Thus they were able to hold the situation until General Knox's brilliantly manoeuvred cannons into place, which is described later in this chapter.

The New Hampshire Regiment was subsequently attached to the Continental Army and Stark was offered a command. This he gratefully accepted and saw action in Canada in 1776 and thereafter at the Battles of Trenton and Princeton. He was later re-commissioned as a Brigadier General of the New Hampshire Militia, answerable to the authority of the Continental Army. He was ordered to reinforce the Continental Army at Saratoga but instead he engaged British Hessians at Bennington. Before the battle, he is quoted as rousing his troops with the words, "There are your enemies, the Red Coats and Tories. They are ours, or this night Molly Stark sleeps a widow." His wife was not a widow, of course but the battle is seen as a turning point of the War.

At the end of the Revolutionary War, John Stark retired and took little part in former officer occasions. When he was invited at the age of 81 to attend a reunion of Bennington veterans, Stark was too unwell to attend, but wrote a letter to those attending the event. It contained the words for which he was to become renowned, "Live free or die: Death is not the worst of evils." In 1945, New Hampshire adopted the words "Live free or die" as its state motto.

John Stark's boyhood home at 2000 Elm Street, Manchester, New Hampshire survives much the same today as it looked when his father Archibald Stark built it in 1736.[2]

## General Henry Knox

General Henry Knox's father, William, was a ship's captain who emigrated from Belfast to Boston in 1729. As his mother Mary was widowed not long after their arrival, young Henry decided to leave school at 12 years of age. Instead of attending college, Knox worked in a bookstore in Boston and shortly afterwards opened his own establishment, in that city. It was known as the 'London Book Store'. Knox always read avidly, particularly on military subjects, and subsequently George Washington took the calculated risk of making him one of his four key Generals during the American Revolution.

His most famous victory was at the Dorchester Heights which overlook

Boston Harbour. Knox, in an audacious and daringly brilliant move, perhaps reminiscent of Hannibal and the elephants, brought 60 tons of cannon across from Fort Ticonderoga in upstate New York to that important vantage point.[4] The weaponry had been abandoned by the British after the French and Indian War, and Knox had it transported on 80 oxen-drawn sleds across dangerous frozen terrain. On the last part of the 300 mile journey, straw was brought from Roxbury, and wrapped around the metal wheels of the cannon so that they could be trundled into place with a minimal amount of noise. The overlooking threat prevented the British fleet from entering Boston, where it really needed to establish a strategic base. Within a few days General Howe, his troops and 1,000 colonial loyalists set sail for Nova Scotia. Knox's in-laws were in fact loyalists and they fled Massachusetts to seek refuge, and sadly Knox's wife never saw them again.

Knox, along with George Washington, was one of those who established the Society of the Cincinnati. It is a Masonic type fraternity, but one where membership is inherited through family rather than elective or open.

Henry Knox later settled at Montpelier near Thomaston, Maine where his home is today a Heritage Centre. When Knox lived there he engaged in ship-building, stock-raising and brick-making, and was not as popular an employer as might be expected, given his heroic war record.

Henry Knox died of peritonitis in 1806 after accidently swallowing a chicken bone. Today there is a Fort Knox in both Maine and Kentucky, the city of Knoxville in Tennessee and nine different states have a Knox County, all named in his honour.[5]

## Botanist, Professor Asa Gray

Asa Gray was born at Sauquoit near Paris, New York in November 1810. He was the great-great-grandson of Matthew Gray of Worcester, Massachusetts and as such was a descendant of the 1718 exodus from Ulster.

He became a Doctor of Medicine in 1831 but decided to give up practising in favour of studying botany. In 1842 he was appointed as Professor of Natural History at Harvard University.

In 1872 and again in 1877, Gray travelled to the American West to carry out botanical research. On the latter trip he collected more than a thousand specimens. A very significant event took place at Kew in London when Gray met Charles Darwin. Darwin subsequently wrote to Gray requesting information about the distribution of various American flowers. Gray's information was very useful in the development of Darwin's Theory of Evolution and they were to enjoy a lifelong collegiate exchange of letters.

Gray argued for conciliation between belief in God and Darwinism. He himself remained a devout Christian all his life and wrote,

> *"I am, scientifically and in my own fashion, a Darwinian, philosophically, a convinced Theist, and religiously, an acceptor of the creed commonly called the Nicene, as the exponent of the Christian faith".*[6]

As well as being elevated to the position of being a Member of the Royal Society of London, more recent recognition was also achieved when the American Society of Plant Taxonomists established the Asa Gray Award in 1984 to honour a living botanist for his career achievements.

Asa Gray died in Cambridge aged 77 and his life was celebrated in these words of the New England poet, James Russell Lowell:

> *Kind Fate, prolong the days well spent,*
> *Whose indefatigable hours*
> *Have been as gaily innocent*
> *And fragrant as his flowers.*[7]

## James Nesmith

Among the first 16 people who settled in Londonderry, New Hampshire in the first tranche was James Nesmith from Londonderry in Ulster. He married Elizabeth McKeen who was originally from Ballymoney, County Antrim. James died in 1767 aged 75 and Elizabeth died in 1763 aged 67.[2] They were the ancestors of Mike Nesmith, who readers of a certain age will have no difficulty identifying as the tall cool one, with the wool hat and sideburns in 1960s fab group 'The Monkees'.

# Endnotes

1. Rev EL Parker, *The History of Londonderry comprising the towns of Derry and Londonderry NH*, a facsimile of the 1851 edition, Londonderry NH, 1934
2. Richard Holmes, *The Road to Derry, A Brief History*, The History Press, Charleston SC, 2009.
3. *The Letters of John and Abigail Adams*, Penguin Classics Edition p250 and 251
4. Authorities differ as to just how many guns were brought from Ticonderoga: Freeman says 66, Spaulding 55, Perry 78; and the Commonwealth of Massachusetts states in its 1925 House Document 219, that there were 58

pieces. The inventory of Knox himself, however, sets the number as 59, as does Flick, which is probably correct.

5. North Callahan, *Henry Knox, General Washington's General*, Rinehart & Company, Inc, 1958
6. 'Asa Gray and the Emergence of Modern Biology', God and Nature Magazine website, http://godandnature.asa3.org/column-time-capsule2.html, date accessed 26 June 2013
7. Rev AL Perry, *Scotch-Irish in New England: Proceedings and Addresses of the Second Congress at Pittsburgh, Pennsylvania, May 29 to June 1, 1890*

# CHAPTER 24

## The Rise and Fall of the McLellan family of Ballymoney and Maine

On 20 August 1720, Bryce McLellan, a weaver from Ulster, presented his credentials from the Presbyterian sessions in Ballymoney, County Antrim to the Congregational Church at Wells Maine. The proprietors of the town granted him ten acres of meadowland. The tough pioneer settlement of Wells had survived the ravages of the ongoing 'Indian Wars' and had just begun to prosper at this time. Since 1652, Maine had been under the political and religious domination of nearby Puritan Massachusetts. As the Puritan Congregational Church was virtually the only available public worship in Wells at the time, Bryce joined the congregation of the patrician Rev Samuel Moody, who was a close friend of the renowned revivalist Jonathan Edwardes. However, Moody is chiefly remembered for having led the attack on the French fort of Louisburg armed with a hatchet, which he referred to somewhat confusingly as "the sword of the Lord and of Gideon".[1]

However, Wells was not the place where Bryce McLellan would make his fortune. His children had become sick there and all had perished save his eldest son Alexander, who had been born in Ballymoney. In 1728, Bryce 'upped sticks' and moved to Casco Bay, where he spent a couple of years in what was then Cape Elizabeth and is today the suburb of South Portland. He moved on again within a couple of years and settled at Falmouth Neck, today the city of Portland, and took up residence close to present day York Street and High Street. The town was then a major 'masting post' for the Royal Navy, largely because of its excellent harbour facilities and the ready availability of timber most suitable for the manufacture of ships' masts. However, it was not yet the significant and wealthy port engaged in world trade that it was later to become. Notwithstanding this, there were already signs of individual merchants striving to acquire finery and elegance.[1]

Initially, Bryce McLellan was a poor but useful and hardworking member of the community. His Portland home was a small cabin, which sat in 2–3 acres of "enclosed and fenced" land. Bryce laid claim to the tidal flats immediately behind his house, which stretched as far as the channel of the river. He did not allow anyone to remove seaweed from or to dig for clams in this area, which he enclosed and on which he then built a 50 foot wharf. Although he had worked in Ulster almost solely as a weaver, Bryce McLellan now offered a variety of 'handyman' skills to the people of Falmouth, largely within the area of farming and labouring. Records show that between 1738 and 1773 he held a number of minor town offices to supplement his pay with other small incomes. It is recorded that he worked as "a constable, a surveyor, a culler of fish, a tything man, and a fence viewer." In 1773 he was awarded £13.04 for "officiating in the smallpox". He was a 'jack of all trades' and his son Alexander was growing up to operate in the same way.[1]

It was in his Falmouth house that Bryce had a new family: Susannah (1731–1812), Captain Joseph (1732–1820), Deacon James (1734–1792), Captain William (1736–1815) and possibly also Margaret, Mary, and Rachel. Of these offspring, Joseph was the most talented and ambitious. Bryce's wife Jane died in the late 1730s and in 1741 he married Elizabeth Miller (1692–1770). At this time there was some tension between Rev Thomas Smith of the First Parish Church in Falmouth and the McLellans who were members of the Congregational Church but nonetheless seemed to be clinging to their Presbyterian ways.[1]

Thirteen years after Bryce's arrival in Maine in 1733, his cousin Hugh and wife Elizabeth left County Antrim and immigrated to York, Maine. The McLellans (Bryce and also Hugh and Elizabeth) were individually descended from Sir Hugh McLellan of Scotland, who had been knighted in 1515. The family were originally lowland Scots, with their main castle being situated in Kirkcudbright. The family had settled in Ulster at the time of the Plantation. When Hugh and Elizabeth married in 1729, however, there was opposition to the match, as Elizabeth's family had developed as the wealthier branch of the clan. Elizabeth was actually disowned by her uncle and this may have been a key factor which prompted the couple's emigration. After staying for a while with his brother James in Saco, Maine, Hugh stayed briefly with Bryce in Falmouth. He pushed on to settle in the frontier township of Narragansett Number 7, which later became known as Gorham. There he purchased 200 acres of land for the princely sum of £15.00, which even then appeared like a remarkable deal until you realise that these were 200 acres of hostile wilderness, where virtually no one else wanted to live. There were no roads, no shops, no governmental services, and a constant and frighteningly real threat of Indian attack. In 1746, the McLellans' nearest neighbour was killed and as a result the family took refuge in the fort at the top of the hill near their cabin. They stayed there for seven years until peace was eventually secured. The family was then able to return to their log cabin. It was at this time that Hugh and Elizabeth began to prosper, farming for sustenance and cutting timber for sale to a growing number of settlers in the area. They coupled this energy with a frugality for which they were to become renowned. They were to have a large family and about 20 years after they moved back to their log cabin, Hugh McLellan spoke about the need to build a home with more space. His actual words are worth noting, as a statement of the ambition and striving will of the Scotch-Irish settlers on this frontier:

> *Your mother has always said when we talked about it that as we both belong to a race that has had lands and lived in stone houses, and as they turned her out of doors for having married a poor man, and we now have more land than any of them, if your mother is to have a new house it should be a brick one.*[2]

Thus the family moved from a one room house to a house with 15 rooms, which was a great talking point in the local vicinity. Elder Hugh as he was known was now the wealthiest man in Gorham and owned 1,500 acres of land, as well as many cattle and slaves. He had achieved all of this because he was prepared from the start to literally tame the wilderness.

Meantime Bryce's sons, Joseph, William and George, all received their maritime training aboard local vessels engaged in the West Indies trade. All of these McLellan sons became master mariners. Joseph purchased his first 'cumpas' (sic) in 1756.[2]

The two branches of the family came together with the marriages of Elder Hugh's daughter Abigail to Deacon James McLellan and her sister Mary to Captain Joseph. Thus the maritime McLellans of Falmouth married into the agricultural McLellans of Gorham. As a result, we see how the McLellan clan came together as described by their son-in-law Rev Elijah Kellogg.

> *Joseph carried lumber to the West Indies and they (the Gorham McLellans) built his vessel, and loaded her from their own forests. They bought timber lands, and on small streams that they could dam with little expense, sawed out their own timber, hauled it with their own teams, and raised their own hay and cattle.*[3]

By 1766, Captain Joseph owned a 54 ton vessel and a quarter share in an 18 ton vessel. Though he continued to call himself a mariner he was now also licensed to sell tea, coffee and chinaware.

At this time, the British viewed Falmouth as a "nest of rebels" and by December 1774, Joseph was appointed as one of a three man team given the task of securing cannon for the defence of the city. At this time the colonial merchants became loosely organised as 'The American Association'. In April 1775, Joseph was appointed by a local committee to obtain gunpowder from Boston and in the following month he was sent to Andover on a similar mission. This kind of venture took time and money to complete but meant that Joseph was well in with the local rebel Popular Party. On 16 October 1775, a British flotilla entered Casco Bay, fired on the town and set fire to a vast area. Joseph McLellan had run his vessel down to the safety of Harpswell at the far end of Casco Bay whilst Mary had sent the children to Gorham to take refuge at Elder Hugh's house.[2]

After the Revolution the McLellans survived the upheaval and began to assume real prominence in the town of Portland. Bryce, the immigrant from Ballymoney, died in March 1776 and thereafter Joseph started to style himself as a 'merchant' rather than a 'mariner'. In 1780, he was commanding officer at Falmouth and when the official end to the war came with the Peace of Paris 1783, the McLellans were poised financially and socially to rise even further. In 1793, the French Republic declared war on Great Britain and America's mercantile trade, including that of the McLellans, benefitted from selling to both sides. When politics started to replace 'the power of the pulpit', the McLellan family prospered even more. At this time, Falmouth experienced an influx of craftsmen, itinerant painters and mechanics, and the development of "banks, insurance companies, lottery offices, libraries, academies, militia units, independent fire companies, stores, wharfs, churches, newspapers and elegant residences".[2]

Slavery was abolished in Massachusetts and in what was then the District of Maine in 1783. Indentured servants now made up most of the workforce and so it was with the McLellans. In this new town (now called Casco Bay) the shipping firm of Joseph McLellan and Son was quite simply "the largest ship owner in Maine" before 1807. The firm was said to be as well known for its trade in Liverpool, England as it was in America. The McLellan shop which was situated on Main (now Congress) Street had by now developed into a large General Store, which operated using barter as well as conventional buying and selling. It also extensively used a system of IOUs, sadly to its detriment in the long run. The firm also hired vessels at this stage to sell

Georgia cotton and moved cargoes between Boston, Charleston (South Carolina) and Liverpool.

They had developed to the zenith of their social and economic power by the time of Jefferson's Embargo Act of 1807. Under its terms no American ship was permitted to sail to foreign ports and no foreign vessel was allowed to unload its cargo at American ports. Until now the McLellans had reached a point whereby they lived in great mansions and were key to the economic life of the town. The third and fourth generation were in the practice of arranging marriages with the other great families in the town. However, the effect of the embargo on trade and the toppling of the 'paper economy' led to consequent bankruptcy and set relative against relative within this once tightly knit Scotch-Irish clan. This is shown by the fact that Rev Elijah Kellogg actually sued his own father-in-law, Joseph McLellan senior.[1]

Symbolically all was lost on 15 June 1810 when Stephen McLellan sold the magnificent McLellan mansion in Portland for $2000 and persuaded the new owner to retain his services as manager of this newly created 'Boarding House'. In the years that followed, occasionally individual members of the McLellan family achieved prominence as State Senator or Judge but by and large their reign was over. The family of Bryce McLellan weaver from Ballymoney, County Antrim had enjoyed fabulous wealth but this had been reversed when the tide was almost literally turned against them by Thomas Jefferson's embargo policy.[1]

## Endnotes

1. William David Barry and John Holverson, 'The Revolutionary McLellans', unpublished thesis in Maine Historical Society, Portland, Maine
2. William David Barry, 'Bryce McLellan and his children', unpublished thesis in Maine Historical Society, Portland, Maine
3. Rev Elijah Kellogg, *Good Old Times or Grandfather's Struggle for a Homestead*, Boston, Lee and Sheperd, 1893

# CHAPTER 25

## Robert Dinsmoor

*The picture painted with words in his poems and letters of Scotch-Irish pioneer settlement in New England*

In 1828 Robert Dinsmoor, 'Rustic Bard' of New Hampshire, published his *Incidental Poems*. Some of these were written in English and some in Ullans, the dialect of the Lowland Scots language of his ancestors.

His father's great-grandfather, John Dinsmoor, had come to County Antrim from Achenmead near the River Tweed in Scotland following a family dispute with his brother. He subsequently settled at Ballywattick, which lies on the Coleraine side of Ballymoney, and the Hearthmoney Rolls show John living there in 1666.

In the 1720s his son (also named John) immigrated to America, not long after the exodus of the Rev McGregor of Macosquin, who led his congregation in the famous 'five ships' that sailed to New England. John, who was known in America as 'Daddy Dinsmoor', settled first in Maine at Fort George. There he enjoyed, as he believed, good relations with his Native American neighbours, whose tribesmen often repeated to him the mantra "All one Brother". Although he was kidnapped by them and held in captivity for three months, the tribesmen's chief befriended him during this period and eventually set him free. He then made his way to the Scotch-Irish settlement of Londonderry, New Hampshire. Many of the inhabitants of that town knew him and he was granted 100 acres by its proprietors. He was a stonemason by trade and so not surprisingly he built a stone house and sent word back to Ballymoney for his wife and children to join him in the New World.

In 1731 his son William was born. William was the father of Robert the poet, who was born in 1757, just two years before the other Robert the poet – Burns of Ayrshire. In an introduction to his work, Dinsmoor tells us that his childhood utterances were quite precocious beyond his years and that his grandfather said about him, "There is something extraordinary in that wean." Surprisingly, Dinsmoor was writing in Scotch before he had even heard of Robert Burns. When he was a lad of 15 he wrote a poem about his pet dog 'Skip', in which he emphasised the sense of equality that he felt there was for all God's creatures:

*Though like a lord man o'er ye rules,*
*An' bang ye round wi' chairs an' stools,*
*An' bruse ye wi' the auld pot buils,*
   *Mind not their powers–*
*Their bodies maun gang to the mools,*
   *As weel as ours.*

Dinsmoor was concerned to write properly in Scotch, to observe its linguistic rules and not to treat it as slang or make up words. Writing to his friend Silas Beton, who was editor of *Haverhill Intelligencer*, he discusses whether 'mools' has a singular form:

*Let not the insignificant term, 'mools' distress you – it passes very well. Mr Allen told me the other day, the poem was well received in Haverhill, and much applauded amongst his readers, as far as he could learn. I think, myself, 'mools' has no singular other than ashes. But this is not discerned by the generality of our Scotch readers – They consider it to mean the same as 'moul', which is pretty generally understood earth or mould, perhaps originating from moulder, as a body mouldering in the dust.*

Quite uniquely amongst Scotch-Irish settlement in America, the Scotch-Irish in Londonderry acted as a reinforcing community of Scots, much in the way the Famine Irish of the mid-nineteenth century strengthened their culture and language. Later Scotch-Irish settlement in America was more individualistic and thus not reinforcing of the culture or language. Interestingly, the community looked to the family of the original leaders, the McGregors and McKeens, for leadership. Writing in 1809 Dinsmoor said, "I am told that Capt Hunter's wife (a McGregore) is the best Scotch dictionary in Londonderry and reads it the best." For this community, speaking Scotch was obviously a living phenomenon. Dinsmoor emphasised this when speaking of his brother, John, as a youngster, "I tried to make the little rascal speak English at first, but I soon found he was far better versed in Scotch."

Robert Dinsmoor also uses Scotch as an everyday parlance rather than as merely a decorous artifice purely for poets. So in one of his letters we see him writing, "It will soon be some wee short hour ayont the twall." (beyond 12 midnight). Nor does Dinsmoor skip out the Ulster experience or somehow make it blander, as is common with some other writers of Scotch-Irish ancestry. In this, the settlers in Londonderry, New Hampshire did not see themselves as having common cause with Catholics against the established Episcopalian Church, and Dinsmoor rails against both Popes and bishops in his writing. Interestingly, he does not perceive speaking in Scotch as a purely insider New England phenomenon. In this respect note the title of this poem:

**The Author to his Friend, Col Silas Dinsmoor, of Mobil, Alabama, in Scotch, the Dialect of their Ancestors**

*Our great grandsire fam'd and rever'd*
*In Londonderry lies interr'd!*
*There, at his head wi' kind regard,*
*    We'd pile some stanes,*
*Renew the turf, and right the swaird,*
*    That co'ers his banes!*

*Whan we our ancient line retrace,*
*He was the first o' a' our race,*
*Cauld Erin ca' his native place,*
*    O' name Dinsmore!*
*And first that saw wi' joyfu' face,*
*    Columbia's shore!*

*Though death our ancestors has cleeket,*
*An' under clods them closely steeket;*
*Their native tongue we yet wad speak it,*
*    Wi' accent glib;*
*And mark the place their chimney's reeket,*
*    Like brithers sib.*

The most famous event in Ulster history is probably the Siege of Derry. My earliest named ancestor was in that siege and so was John Mann's, from Maine, who wrote the Foreword to this book. Indeed, many of today's Maine population's ancestors may have been there too. Everyone in Londonderry, New Hampshire had either been at the siege or was the son, daughter, grandson or granddaughter of one of those inside Derry in the winter of 1688/9. Rev McGregor as a ten year old boy had rung the bell in St Columb's Cathedral when *The Mountjoy* broke the boom that was placed across the River Foyle.

Dinsmoor's take on that event, which touches on Derry, fighting the Indians and the American Revolution may be found brought together in his poem *Antiquity – The Auld Gun*.

Although Dinsmoor wrote in Scotch and had a proud awareness of his ancestry, he was never imitative or sentimental about either Scotland or Ulster. Burns' work inspired him but his work had an honesty about it and he did not pretend to be anywhere else than he found himself. John Greenleaf Whittier said of him:

> *"Burns is the bonny Doon flowing through the banks and braes of Scotland, and Dinsmoor is the Merrimack passing through our western soil and reflecting from its crystal bed the western scenery through which it passes."*

Dinsmoor supported the Revolutionary cause from an early age. At 18 he was "a fifer in Captain Reynolds' company" and "At twenty [he] was at the taking of Burgoyne". In the lines that he addressed to 'Lt David Gregg on the Return of the Soldiers from Bennington' he portrays Windham by Londonderry as an entirely committed patriot centre:

> *On every side I hear a cheerful sound,*
> *Gladness and mirth this morning doth abound.*

Dinsmoor was never in doubt about where his allegiance might lie and in this poem for Isaac Cochran, his mother's brother and a fellow soldier, his writing expressed the enthusiasm that he and others felt for the American cause:

> *When British laws would us enthral,*
> *Our country for defence did call;*
> *Then martial fire inspir'd us all,*
>     *To arms we flew;*
> *And as a soldier, stand or fall,*
>     *I went with you!*

John Steinbeck and others have stressed the ready ability of the Scotch-Irish to tackle any challenge that arose in making items of wood or metal and a marvellous dexterity that surprises today, given the very basic nature of the tools available at that time. Dinsmoor's remarks about his father ring true about Scotch-Irish on the frontier, where more than most other nationalities, they made a virtue out of necessity: "He began the world with little more than his land. He was a wonderful mechanical genius, and made all the wooden utensils both for his house and farm".

Also noteworthy is this core necessity to own land. The ties of family and community were strong in Londonderry. Robert Dinsmoor writes of the kindness afforded to him by a kinsman, demonstrating the generosity shown to one another by the pioneer community, and furthermore the very crucial importance that chopping and selling of firewood had for early settlers on the New England frontier. An incident occurred just before Dinsmoor's first wife died when he was at low ebb.

> *A few evenings before her departure, he came to see her, and privately put a thirty dollar bill into my hands, saying, 'Robin if you stand in need use that freely.'*
>
> *It was a great kindness to me at that time, and I hope never to forget it. Fortunately by the sale of a boat load of wood at Newbury, I was enabled to return it to him ...*

For many Scotch-Irish emigrants the biggest push factor was a lack of fundamental freedoms in Ulster.

> *And where our fathers long had been,*
> *By Lords and bishops press'd.*

More than that, Dinsmoor reflects the view that, for many Scotch-Irish settlers, New England was the Promised Land to which they had been delivered:

> *New Hampshire's sons, with plenty blest,*
> *May by their social fireside stay,*
> *By no fell tyrant's hand opprest,*
> *'Till winter's storms have howled away.*

Not only the Promised Land but also the Land of Milk and Honey, as here in *The Frosted Corn*.

> *Then smiling wives wi' a' their brood,*
> *Shall grace our board in jovial mood,*
> *An' wi' us sup the luscious food,*
>     *Like Yankees true,*
> *Syne we will praise the name o' Gude,*
> *When we are fu'.*

Always one finds that Robert Dinsmoor combined a sense of lurking danger on the frontier with a degree of humour almost as a defence mechanism. In one letter he writes about the irregular lessons that he received from the village schoolmaster, McKeen:

> *He was a man of profound erudition, but very dilatory in attending. If he took in hand to catch a squirrel by the way, he would do it if it took him half the forenoon.*

Also Dinsmoor tells how Skip his pet dog had a role in protecting the community's interest and was one of those dogs that liked to join in with sacred observance, particularly if it was of a musical nature:

> *He tried to keep the corn frae bears,*
> *An' help'd us ay to sing our prayers.*

If they sang Metrical Psalms it would be interesting to know if the sounding of the tuning fork was the signal for Skip to commence his role as chanter.

Dinsmoor reveals just how much of being literate at that place and time was for him tied up with being a Presbyterian. In one letter, he reveals that although he did not go to school until he was nine years of age, within two years he had mastered language skills that were quite developed by any measure.

> *At the age of eleven years, I could repeat the Shorter Catechism and Longer Catechism verbatim. Those with the scripture proofs annexed to them confirmed me in the orthodoxy of my forefathers.*

The letter further discloses that he was an elder in the church before he was 30 years of age. Thus we come to see him as a member of a society that engages in lively philosophical discussion about religious doctrine and preaching:

> *Then in my field we would dispute 'im,*
> *And sometimes we would laugh and hoot 'im,*
> *And three miles off we could refute 'im,*
>   *With reasons strong,*
> *And with false doctrines durst impute 'im,*
>   *And tenets wrong.*

Famously he advised Rev David McGregor (see Chapter 23) as to how to deal with Unitarian opposition to Trinitarian Orthodox Presbyterians:

*When Unitarian champions dare thee,*
*Goliah like, and think to scare thee,*
*Dear Davie, fear na', they'll no waur ye;*
    *But, draw thy sling,*
*Weel loaded, frae the Gospel quarry,*
    *Syne gie't a fling.*

Although Dinsmoor as a young man was writing in Scotch before he ever heard of Robert Burns, it is obvious that in later life Burns did inspire him, both in his sensibility embracing equality, and in his style of writing. He explained this in a letter to Silas Burns, in which he described how he came to write a poem called *The Sparrow*.

*It was occasioned by my crushing a nest of sparrow's eggs when I was ploughing among the corn, July 20, 1812. And about that time saw a well done piece in the Haverhill Intelligencer, in imitation of Burns' delightful Nanny, which induced me to adopt the Scottish dialect, that it might the better resemble his beautiful mountain daisy – I call it The Sparrow.*

In this poem Dinsmoor starts to play around again with the words 'moul' and 'mouldering'.

*Poor innocent and hapless Sparrow!*
*Why should my moul-board gie thee sorrow?*
*This day thou'll chirp an' mourn the morrow,*
    *Wi' anxious breast–*
*The plough has turn'd the mould'ring furrow*
    *Deep o'er thy nest.*

*How much like theirs are human dools*
*Their sweet wee bairns laid I' the mools*

Such is the affection that Dinsmoor feels for Burns that he writes about what it might be like to meet his kindred spirit:

*'Could I, O Rab, but brak' my tether,*
*An' ony whar' wi' you forgether,*

*I'm sure we'd souple baith our leather,*
  *I'd lay my lugs,*
*We'd mak' our hearts as light's a fether,*
  *Wi' reaming jugs.*

And so Dinsmoor's New England emerges as a hardscrabble place where the threat from Indians, wolves and bears is very real. However, it was also a place where the sons and grandsons of those who had suffered inside the Siege of Derry had wrapped around their new urban community a belief in a God who had delivered them, against all odds, to a land flowing with milk and honey, where there was immediate rapport and sustained comfort in the music and inflexion of their mother tongue.

# Reference

*Robert Dinsmoor's Scotch-Irish Poems*, Introduced by Frank Ferguson and Alister McReynolds, Ulster Historical Foundation, Belfast, 2012

### John Greenleaf Whittier to the 'Rustic Bard'
*(Whittier, a Quaker hymn writer and poet, was a personal friend of Robert Dinsmoor)*

*Health to the hale auld 'Rustic Bard'!*
*Gin ye a poet wad regard,*
*Who deems it honor to be ca'd*
*Yere rhymin' brither,*
*'Twould gie his muse a rich reward–*
*He asks nae ither.*
*My muse, an inexperienced hizzie,*
*Wi' pride an' self-importance dizzy,*
*O' skill to rhyme it, free an' easy,*
*Is na possessor;*
*But yours has been a lang time busy–*
*An auld transgressor.*
*Yes, lang an' weel ye've held your way,*
*An' spite o' a' that critics say,*
*The memory of your rustic lay,*
*Shall still be dear;*
*And wi' yere name to latest day,*
*Be cherish'd here.*

# CHAPTER 26

## Agents Temple and Dunbar

*The work of 'Settlement Agents' in developing Scotch-Irish settlements in Maine*

### Robert Temple and the 'lost' Scotch-Irish settlement of Cork, Maine, New England

Robert Temple was born in Ireland in 1694. He was not himself Scotch-Irish, as is sometimes stated. His great-grandfather died in Ireland in 1671 but had actually been born in Warwickshire, came to Ireland with Cromwell's army and was apportioned land in County Tipperary in 1653. From there the family also spread to Cork and Kerry. Robert, as you might guess, is thought to have been of the Cork branch.

At a later period, when living in Charlestown, Massachusetts, Robert Temple had six slaves, four of whom he named: Bandon, Mallow, Kerry and Limerick. This perhaps suggests why he might have decided to call the area of Maine which he planted 'Cork', since he obviously had considerable affection for the part of Ireland that he came from.

We can learn about Temple's motivation and objectives from his own account, which is contained in a letter of 1753 to 'The Plymouth Proprietors'. It explains how he came to America in 1717, with his "servants and effects". He was aged just 23 when he landed in Boston and we are told that he conceived "the idea of establishing himself as a great landed proprietor in America." That ambition was very much a live possibility at the time, as two years before a number of landed proprietors known as the Pejebscot Company had laid the foundation of several towns in the Sagadahoc Peninsula and the northeast shore of the Kennebec/Georgetown region. Here, Temple met with Col Thomas Hutchinson and other members of the Company. He agreed to act as their agent in transplanting immigrants and settling them on lands on the Kennebec River.

Temple then returned to Ireland and there he immediately chartered two "large ships" (his words), and in the next year three more ships, in which to bring out about 200 families from Ulster. They landed in the Kennebec River area. According to Temple himself, the majority of that group went to Pennsylvania and Londonderry, New Hampshire "for fear of the Indians, who were very troublesome at that time."[1] He also says that he "settled some families on the east side of Merrymeeting Bay, to which we gave the name of Cork." He then received a further 1,000 acres on the 'Chops' of Merrymeeting Bay, named by Col Winthrop as 'Temple Bar'. Robert Temple modestly points out that he would have been embarrassed to name it after himself or his family.[1]

The settlement consisted of a cluster of log homes in what is now called Hatche's Corner in the town of Dresden, where the Eastern River and the Kennebec meet. The Cork settlement had a garrison 'castle', wherein Temple himself lived. Predictably the local Native American tribes were not happy. They threatened to massacre all the settlers with particular umbrage being directed against the agent. They issued a threat to all who lived in 'Summerset', which had been named by prominent settler Andrew McFadden. He called it after his home, Somerset Woods in Coleraine, which still today lies close to the Cutts on the River Bann.[2]

As a response to the threat, troops were dispatched from Swan Island and Cork. The provocation caused by further incursions in to Indian hunting grounds resulted in a murderous campaign in 1722. Indians swept down through the valley and killed and burned out settlers, and killed or drove off cattle. As a result, the settlers sought refuge but there was little shelter to be had. Temple 'hung on' and was still there in 1722 with just 56 troops in his guard. By 1724, even he had suffered enough and Cork was abandoned. The cove in which Cork stood still exists today. In 1757, German settlers moved in and renamed it as Dresden. Robert Temple moved to Boston and bought a farm at Ten Hills, Charlestown, where he lived for the next 26 years. He died there in 1754.[2]

## Colonel David Dunbar in Maine

Col David Dunbar was born in Hingham, Massachusetts in 1704, into a family that was well-established in New England. Both his mother and father were also born there, with his mother's people, the Gardener family, who had come there with the Pilgrim Fathers.

In 1728, Dunbar was made Surveyor General of the King's Woods "in America and Nova Scotia". In that role he was tasked with providing supplies and resources for the British Navy, particularly in Maine the white pine tree, the trunks of which were much prized by shipbuilders for 'masting' purposes.

In 1729, following 30 years of dispute between the British and the Massachusetts authorities over who was responsible for rebuilding Pemaquid Fort (otherwise known as Fort William Henry), destroyed in 1696, Col David Dunbar arrived. He announced that he had a Royal Commission to set up a new state separate from Massachusetts, which was to be called Sagadahoc. This was conceived as being a separate province in the area between the Kennebec and the St Croix rivers. He rebuilt the fort and renamed it Fort Frederick in honour of the Prince of Wales of the day. Obviously the Massachusetts authorities were not happy about this and Dunbar constantly feared attack from that quarter.[3]

To help him in his quest, Dunbar brought in Scotch-Irish settlers, including interrelated clans of families from County Tyrone and County Antrim in the period between 1729 and 1731.[4] Other settlers were brought up from Londonderry, New Hampshire and Pennsylvania. The group in Pennsylvania were initially from the Boston area but were taking temporary refuge in Pennsylvania to escape the ill-treatment meted out to them by the Bostonian Puritan hierarchy. He described them as "a great many hundred men of those who came lately from Ireland". Although he felt he might need their help against the Massachusetts authorities, for whom many of the settlers had no love, his main intention was to use these people as a buffer against the Abenaki St Francis Native American allies of the French authorities. He planned to offer each settler between 50 and 100 acres of land. He described the people as being "originally from North Britain but last from Ireland."

Dunbar had Royal approval for his actions. In 1729, in the same month as Dunbar was rebuilding Fort Frederick, the King ordered Massachusetts Governor Jonathan Belcher specifically not to undertake,

> *"a military expedition against Frederick's Fort formerly called the Fort of Pemaquid in order to remove several Irish Protestants lately settled upon certain lands there by Colonel Dunbar."*

Belcher of course explained that the thought never crossed his mind.

Once the fort was rebuilt, Dunbar proceeded to establish settlements that were populated principally by Scotch-Irish on both sides of the Damariscotta River. Amongst these settlements was Townsend, formerly known as Winnegance. The most prominent Scotch-Irish settler there was a man called Samuel McCobb. It was never going to be a smooth operation and there were numerous complaints, including a formal hearing and decision by the Board of Trade that the Crown did not have jurisdiction over Sagadahoc and that control had passed to Massachusetts. So Dunbar was dismissed in August 1732 and left Pemaquid permanently in 1734. The remaining Scotch-Irish settlers were left 'high and dry'. They had settled on the Damariscotta River and had been promised title deeds which were to be enacted by the Governor of nearest British jurisdiction, ie Nova Scotia. That never happened and it is doubtful if it ever would have taken place. In 1738, Dunbar sought and received compensation in London, although it was concluded he had 'overstepped the mark'. [3]

For the people who had come from Ulster, the risk of attack by Native American tribes was nonetheless worthwhile if the alternative was poverty. Numerous Scotch-Irish of later times were relatively 'well-off' but many of the group that Dunbar brought out were in a poor state of physical being and dressed in ragged clothes. A further problematic situation was that Dunbar had declared various parcels of land as 'common'. For example, he ruled that 40 feet from any shore in the area was to be deemed 'common' to all fishermen, and also meadows "up to the rocks in the Damariscotta River granted to said settlers in common". Notwithstanding his settlement shortcomings, Dunbar held on to his role as Surveyor General of the King's Woods and Fort Frederick was maintained until 1759. However, it was subsequently destroyed by locals in 1775, as they were afraid that the British might use it as a base during the American Revolutionary War.

It is clear that the power of agents to place people where they wanted was more limited than perhaps even they themselves realised. Above all, the violent reprisal power, resultant from disrupting and displacing Indian patterns of life and the struggles that were starting to manifest between the British and their colonial authorities was too powerful a discouragement for agents to overcome.

# Endnotes

1. George Varney, 'History of Kennebec County Maine', in Geo J Varney, *A Gazetter of the State of Maine*, BB Russell, Boston, 1886, http://history.rays-place.com/me/kennebec-cty.htm, date accessed 26 April 2013
2. Rebecca Graham, *The Cork settlement of Merrymeeting Bay*, http://www.maineulsterscots.com/docs/CorkArticle.pdf, date accessed 26 April 2013

3. 'Fort Frederick at Pemaquid', Maine.gov website, https://maine.gov/doc/parks/programs/history/pemaquid/fortfred.htm, date accessed 26 April 2013
4. 'The Waldo Patent', Penobscot Marine Museum Education Website, http://penobscotmarinemuseum.org/pbho-1/our-maine-ancestors/waldo-patent, date accessed 26 April 2013

# Reference

Ed Joseph Conforti, *Creating Portland: History and place in Northern New England*, New Hampshire, 1997

Federal Writers' Project of the Works Progress Administration for the State of Maine, *Maine: A Guide 'Down East'*, Houghton Mifflin Company, Boston

Michael C Bratinski, *Jonathan Belcher: Colonial Governor*, University Press of Kentucky, 1996

# CHAPTER 27

## Abolitionist Anthony Benezet quotes two Ulster Scots in support of his argument against slavery, but all may not be as it seems

Anthony Benezet was born in St Quentin France in 1713. When he was still an infant his family fled from France where they had been persecuted as Protestant Huguenots in what was a predominantly Catholic country. The family relocated to London in 1715. There is a distant Ulster connection: Anthony Benezet was a descendant of Armand Crommelin, who was also the ancestor of Louis Crommelin who founded the seventeenth century Huguenot colony in the Lagan Valley around Lisburn.

In 1731 the Benezet family moved again, this time to Philadelphia, the city founded by Quaker William Penn. Anthony himself had become a member of the Society of Friends in London when he was just 14 years of age.

Anthony Benezet became a teacher, opening the first school in America for blacks, uniquely for the time, including girls as pupils. He had strong feelings against slavery and wrote about it extensively and with great passion. One of his better known works on the subject was entitled *A Short Account of that part of Africa, Inhabited by the Negroes*. The book cited the words of other writers that Benezet assumed had supported the abolitionist cause, including Sir Hans Sloane of Killyleagh, Co Down and Francis Hutcheson, born in nearby Saintfield and also educated in Killyleagh. However, it now appears that Sloane's account may not have been written with the sentiment that Benezet assumed it to contain.[1]

In his *History of Jamaica*, as quoted by Benezet, Sloane described how,

> "a rebellious Negroe, or he that twice strikes a white man, is condemned to the flames; being chained flat on his belly, at the place of execution, and his arms and legs extended, fire is then set to his feet, and he is burnt gradually up to his head."

Understandably Benezet and others, such as Dr Benjamin Rush and John Wesley, took this graphic description to be self-evidently repugnant to any educated and morally responsible person. More particularly so, when Sloane added, "they starve others to death, with a loaf hanging before their mouths, so that some gnaw the very flesh off their shoulders." Further description is given of how 'order' was maintained on the sugar plantations when Sloane revealed, "for crimes of a lesser nature, they geld the offender, and chop off half of his foot with an ax; for negligence only, they whip him till his back is raw, and then scatter pepper and salt on his wounds, to heighten the smart, and some planters will drop melted wax on their skins."[1]

Sloane first made the voyage to Jamaica between 1687 and 1689, as personal physician to Charles Monck, Duke of Albemarle. The latter died within months of arrival and Sloane was left with plenty of time to 'discover' chocolate and quinine bark, both of which proved to be lucrative patents when he sold them on, most notably milk chocolate, which he sold to the Cadbury family.

He collected many artefacts which still today form the core of the collection of the British Museum. These included "a barbary scourge with which the slaves are beaten made ... (from) a palm tree"; a "noose made of cane splitt for catching game or hanging runaway negroes"; and a strap "for whipping the negro slaves in the hott W India plantations."

The clue to Sloane's attitude about the rights and wrongs of those 'hott' plantations is revealed by his later marriage to Elizabeth Rose, widow of Dr Fulke Rose, who had owned just such a plantation. Sloane thereby gained access to one third of the income from her late husband's estates and was thus a beneficiary by marriage to an income from plantations worked by slaves.[2]

Professor James Delbourgo of McGill University in Montreal has made a close study of Sloane's time in Jamaica and the 'curiosities' he brought home. He also examined his account books, which show numerous deliveries of sugar from Jamaica. Delbourgo's essay 'Slavery in the Cabinet of Curiosities: Hans Sloane's Atlantic World' revealed how in December 1721 *The Neptune*, a South Sea Company ship, left London for Jamaica with 395 slaves on board. They were en route from the mouth of the River Congo to Jamaica and when that ship returned in April 1723, Sloane's account books detailed a delivery, two days after *Neptune's* docking, of eight hogsheads of sugar worth £32, a figure of greater value when inflated to present day currency.[2]

So given the graphic descriptions cited earlier in this chapter, how could that be Sloane's position? Delbourgo presents a very plausible explanation:

> *In fact his account has most often been seen as highly critical of slavery's excesses. This however, is a misreading of an ambiguous text, one that spoke about slavery not as a matter of moral concern or racialised scientific fact but, most fundamentally, as one of curiosity – a mode of engagement with the natural and social world that generated as many questions as answers.*

Delbourgo explains that "slavery was not yet under concerted attack from abolitionist campaigners, there was no need to defend the institution, even for one with a direct financial stake in it." He reveals that elsewhere Hans Sloane referred to negroes in general as a "very perverse generation of people". In general, Delbourgo portrays Hans Sloane's graphic description of the punishment of black slaves as an account in which "meticulous curiosity drives the passage: a precise observation of the material practices of punishment and their visible bodily effects." In other words, the description which Anthony Benezet had characterised as 'shocking', was actually a cold, scientifically objective description of what happens to the human body when it is subjected to physical trauma. That level of detail was not to be confused with moral outrage and should certainly never get in the way of turning a profit in sugar-cane production.[2]

As regards the other Ulster-Scot quoted by Anthony Benezet, Professor Francis Hutcheson, there is little by way of ambiguity.

Francis Hutcheson's abhorrence of slavery was firmly based from first principles on the Old Testament. Hutcheson expounded clearly on how,

> "the Jewish laws had great regard to Justice, about the servitude of Hebrews, finding it only on consent or some crime or damage, allowing them always a proper redress upon any cruel treatment; and fixing a limited time for it…"

He developed the point with respect to Christianity, based on the New Testament, wherein the Christian message is not just for the Jews, but rather is one for all the peoples of the earth:

> *But under Christianity, whatever Lenity was due from an Hebrew towards his country man must be due toward all; since the distinctions of nations are removed, as to the point of Humanity and Mercy, as well as natural rights.*[3]

Hutcheson then developed this concept of 'natural rights' further by countering an argument in favour of slavery that was current in his time. The argument was that slave traders saved the lives of those they captured, since they would almost certainly have been killed in internecine wars in Africa: "It's pleaded that, in some barbarous nations unless the captives were brought for slaves they would all be murthered (sic)." Hutcheson countered this quite easily by pointing out that doctors, midwives and surgeons often save people's lives, but that that did not entitle them to subsequently enslave their patients.[3]

Hutcheson's clear moral repugnance of slavery cannot be read without thinking of how his words would sit with the true position of that other 'son of Co Down', Sir Hans Sloane:

*Strange that in any nation where a sense of liberty prevails, where the Christian religion is professed, custom and high prospects of gain can so stupefy the conscience of men, and all sense of natural justice, that they can hear such computations made about the value of their fellow-men and their liberty, without abhorrence and indignation.*[3]

This writer would never have stumbled across the clearly different moral stance of the two Ulster-Scots, had not Anthony Benezet quoted both in his book setting out arguments highlighting man's inhumanity to man in the context of Plantation slavery.

## Endnotes

1. Anthony Benezet, *A Short Account of that Part of Africa, Inhabited by the Negroes*, 1762
2. Professor James Delbourgo, 'Slavery in the Cabinet of Curiosities: Hans Sloane's Atlantic World', http://www.britishmuseum.org/PDF/Delbourgo%20essay.pdf, date accessed 23 April 2013
3. Francis Hutcheson, *A System of Moral Philosophy*, 1755

# CHAPTER 28

## Where Scotch-Irish history and culture can be visited in America today

**A suggested Scotch-Irish history trail along the Great Wagon Road with some explanatory notes**

The Great Philadelphia Wagon Road was taken over from a path made by the Iroquois Native American tribes. It had been their 'Ancient Warrior's Path', which they had used either to trade or to fight in Virginia or the Carolinas.

The Scotch-Irish started pouring into this area from the 1740s onwards. These people were nearly all Presbyterian. They were restless, often simply squatting on the land that they acquired. It was said that no Scotch-Irish family felt comfortable until it had moved at least twice. This might have been of necessity since Governor Dobbs of North Carolina, himself a Carrickfergus man, declared that as many as 10,000 immigrants had landed in Philadelphia in a single season, so that many were "obliged to remove to the southward for want of lands to take up" in Pennsylvania. Not only was land scarce in Pennsylvania but it was also expensive. For example, a 50 acre farm in Pennsylvania would cost £7.10 shillings, whereas in the Granville District of North Carolina at the same time, 5 shillings would buy 100 acres. The majority of Scotch-Irish entering America at this time did so through Philadelphia, Chester or Newcastle. Eventually 250,000 would come and settle in the New World. Most would enter by Philadelphia, where the Quaker proprietors were more tolerant and welcoming than the New England Puritans had been in Boston with the earlier exodus from Ulster from 1718.

Along this trail a landscape was constructed consisting of endless farms with the occasional tavern, fort or village. By 1765 the Road was widened for horse-drawn vehicles and maintained. The wagons grew larger, with the famous Conestoga Wagon reaching dimensions of 26 feet long and 11 feet high. Although they were seen as being a devoutly religious people, it was also said of them that they "Kept God's Commandments and everything else that they could get their hands on." As they moved, they lived by hunting and 'slash and burn' agriculture.

When the American Revolution came along, the Scotch-Irish were solidly behind the 'Patriot Cause'. As a ballad of the time said:

*And when the days of trial came,*
*Of which we know the story,*
*No Erin son of Scotia's blood,*
*Was ever found a Tory.*[1]

**Winchester, Virginia** is of course famous as the birthplace of Patsy Cline. It was also one of the places where the Scotch-Irish in the Union army fought against the Scotch-Irish in the Confederate forces. The town today boasts the 'New Museum of the Shenandoah Valley', which tells the story of the Appalachian/Scotch-Irish of the Great Valley.

**Strasburg Museum** features the work and equipment of Scotch-Irish farms in Virginia.

**Staunton, Virginia** houses the museum of the frontier, which is the sister organisation of the Ulster American Folk Park, near Omagh, County Tyrone. It is also the Presbyterian manse which was the boyhood home of President Woodrow Wilson (Strabane), who famously once told a Scotch-Irish audience, "I believe as you do that we actually built this country."

**Wade's Mill, Raphine** is a working water-powered grist mill built in 1750 by a Scotch-Irish family.

**Steeles Tavern, Virginia** was the home of Cyrus McCormick's farm and workshop. His great-grandfather immigrated from Dergina near Ballygawley, County Tyrone and settled initially in Pennsylvania in the 1730s. Cyrus' mother Polly could trace her line back to County Armagh in the late 1640s. Cyrus was born in 1809 and showed an inventive precocity early in life. On his Virginia farm he invented a lightweight cradle for harvesting grain, when he was aged just 15 years of age. Inventing and tinkering with machinery was something that the family generally engaged in, although when Cyrus' father found that he could not complete work on a prototype horse-drawn reaper he handed the project completely over to young Cyrus. Cyrus completed and improved the invention, much-helped by his Negro employee companion and friend, Jo Anderson. By 1849 the company manufacturing the reapers had moved to Chicago and were selling 1,500 reapers per year. By 1859 the figure for annual sales was in the region of 4,100 reapers each year. By now Cyrus McCormick was a millionaire a number of times over.

**Lexington** is famous as the birthplace of Sam Houston who had Ballycarry antecedents and was commander of the Texas army which won the Battle of San Jacinto and achieved Texas' independence. He later became Senator and Governor of Texas. Campbell House tells the story of the Scotch-Irish of Rockbridge County (Rockbridge and Augusta were the most Scotch-Irish of Virginia's counties). The town also contains the house of Stonewall Jackson who taught at the nearby College.

**Big Stone Gap, Tazewell County, Southwest Virginia** contains the Historic Crab Orchard Museum and Pioneer Park, which focus on the history of Southwest Virginia through exhibits of the Revolutionary and the Civil Wars, the tools of Scotch-Irish coal miners and by portraying the agriculture and homelife of the Scotch-Irish in this area.

**Maple Grove Presbyterian Church, Abingdon, Southwest Virginia** was where the Scotch-Irish first established the Presbyterian Church in Southwest Virginia in 1728. They originally called it Springfield.

§

**Birth of Country and Old Timey Music**

**Bristol, Tennessee/Virginia** is where the Carter family made their first recording in 1927. The Carter family are sometimes said to have been the originators of 'Country Music'. At other times the accolade is given to Scotch-Irish Jimmie Rodgers, who was known as the 'Singing Brakeman' and hailed from **Mississippi.**

Over the 17 years that followed, the Carters recorded over 300 ballads, many of which were Scotch-Irish in origin. The original group consisted of Alvin Pleasant, 'AP' Carter, his wife Sara Dougherty Carter and his sister-in-law Maybelle Addington Carter, who was a cousin of Sara. Sara's father was William Sevier Dougherty, from County Tyrone, who was Scotch-Irish and descended from a famous Scottish rebel called William Lawson. Sara's mother was Nancy Elizabeth Kilgore, who was descended from Robert Kilgore, a Revolutionary War veteran who was born in Fife, Scotland, but emigrated from County Clare, Ireland.

**Clinch River, Southwest Virginia** was first settled by a Scotch-Irishman named Thomas McCulloch, who built a home at Fort Houston near Big Moccasin Creek in 1769. An African American called Lesley Riddle grew up in the region, in Kingsport near Bristol. He was an early influence on the Carters musically, bringing them many Scotch-Irish ballads. Among those early tunes that bear the marks of their Scotch-Irish origins were *Wildwood Flower, Keep on the Sunny Side* and *Will the Circle be Unbroken?*

Also from this region, more contemporary but of the same tradition, are Dr Ralph Stanley and the Clinch Mountain Boys, who shot to fame after the movie *O Brother Where Art Thou?*

**Coeburn, near Dungannon, Virginia** is where Jim and Jesse McReynolds and the Virginia Boys originally hailed from. Their grandfather Charles McReynolds and his brother William recorded at that same original Bristol session as the Carters back on Monday 1 August 1927. They styled themselves as 'The Bull Mountain Moonshiners' and along with Howard Green, Charlie Greer and Bill Dean they recorded a version of *Johnny Goodwin* or *The Girl I left Behind Me*. Jim and Jesse had many hits and were early inductees into the Grand Old Opry. Jesse's cross-picking mandolin playing and compositions such as *Dixie Hoedown* have been described as, 'legendary'. Having sadly lost his brother Jim to cancer in 2002, Jesse currently runs 'The Pick Inn' in Gallatin, Tennessee and is keeping the tradition alive with the next generation of the family.

One of Jesse's grandsons, Luke McKnight, who is vocalist and guitarist with 'The McReynolds Tradition', told this writer/kinsman that love of their heritage runs deep in the family and has been much reinforced by the families that the McReynolds clan have married into: "Jim and Jesse McReynolds married McCoy sisters, my mother Gwen McReynolds married a McKnight, and also I married a McKelvey."

**Dandridge, Tennessee** runs the Old Time Main Street Music Festival, which honours the town's earliest settlers in 1783. The town is the second oldest city in Tennessee and was named for the First Lady, Martha Dandridge Washington. The town is found in Jefferson County, Tennessee, which is where David Crockett spent his early adult life. It was here that he married Polly Finlay, who was the first of his two wives.

**Pigeon Forge, Tennessee** is the home of Dollywood, owned by entertainer Dolly Parton and Herschend Family Entertainment. Dolly Rebecca Parton (said to be a version of Patton) was the fourth of 12 children born of 'Scotch-Irish sharecroppers'. Dolly has great 'crossover' appeal and is a Grammy Award-winning singer-songwriter, author, actress and philanthropist. Many of her songs, such as *Tennessee Mountain Home* and *Coat of Many Colours* evoke a childhood that was short on material benefits but big on family and belonging. Her literacy and books programme, called Imagination Library (more than 2.5 million books distributed free annually), could be seen as echoing back to her Scotch-Irish antecedents' love of reading and learning.

# Endnotes

1. 'The Scotch Irish in the Revolution', Philadelphia Reflections website, http://www.philadelphia-reflections.com/blog/1149.htm, date accessed 26 June 2013

**Reeds Valley Virginia – The Fall**

*Only a pile of boards*
*And the well remains*
*Reflecting the brown and orange and yellow*
*From the maple and the hickory*
*The sinister 'conkers' of black walnuts*
*Lie all around like grapeshot.*

*'One of your kin,'*
*My guide informs me,*
*'Hid from the Yankees*
*When they came through*
*During the Civil War*
*Up in a cave in the hills there*
*Spent his time weaving baskets*
*Into all kinds of shapes,'*
*It seems he made*
*A kind of slipe*
*To pull behind the horse*
*And carry four children in.*

*Predictably I feel at home here*
*Where these country folk*
*Kept bees, grew tobacco*
*And were baptised*
*Close by in the Clinch River.*

*Alister J McReynolds*

# ACKNOWLEDGEMENTS

Thanks are due to:

Eileen and the kids for their 100% support.

Ian Carlisle for allowing me to re-use the New England material that has appeared in publications that he commissioned originally.

Bill Barry for allowing me access to his unpublished theses that were so valuable in telling the McLellan story.

John Mann for introducing me to the writings of Rev Elijah Kellogg.

John Wilson for the leads and prompts dispensed at our regular coffee sessions.

Andrew Kennedy for allowing me to use much of the Lisburn material earmarked for history trailing.

Ian Hunter for being so supportive at my speaking engagements.

Bernard Gillialand for his hospitality in Marietta.

Rebecca Graham for access to documents in Maine which otherwise would have been difficult to obtain.

Sammy McReynolds for explaining the essence of the Scotch-Irish in Mississippi.

Johnny and Kay McReynolds for their hospitality in Starkville and John in particular for taking me to Tupelo to see Elvis' homeplace.

Carole and Frank Davis for artwork and explaining Southern political realities.

Luke McKnight for recognition of his heritage and for allowing me to quote his network of family linkages.

Wilfrid Dilworth for Co Tyrone lore and information.

Victor Blease for teaching me to believe in myself.

Ron Rash for allowing me to quote his insight into the Scotch-Irish in the Carolinas.

William Martin Wiseman for his insight into the Reformed Presbyterian Church in North Mississippi.

William Dinsmore of Gortin, Kilrea for valuable information about his ancestor Robert Dinsmoor.

Ian Crozier and all at the Ulster Scots Agency for all their support and for honouring me by asking me to give the 2013 Whitelaw Reid Lecture.

Joe Kennedy for making me aware of the Moira and Trummery connection to James Logan and for being such a fine Quaker gentleman.

My parents Tom and Jean for their patience with my quirky otherworldness.

# INDEX

Illustrations referred to as: *Section One/Two*
References to poems in (brackets)

Abbeville, South Carolina, 20
Abenaki St Francis Indians, 90, 110
Adrain, Robert, 16-17, *Section One*
Aghadowey, Co Londonderry, 85
Allison, Rev Francis, 14, 28
American Revolutionary War, 14-15, 20, 28-29, 31, 62, 75, 90-91, 98, 103, 111, 118, 119, 120
Ardstraw, Co Tyrone, 59-60
Asheville, North Carolina, 62, 63
Atlanta, Georgia, 69

Ballykelly, Co Londonderry, 19, 65-68, *Section Two*
Ballymagorry, Co Tyrone, 59
Ballymena, Co Antrim, 17, 28, 30
Ballymoney, Co Antrim, 13, 93, 95, 98, 99, 100
Ballywattick, Co Antrim, 100
Baltimore, Maryland, 28, 29, 30, 33, 37, 63, 89
Bardstown, Kentucky, 53
Battle of,
    Belmont, 49
    Bennington, 91, 103
    Bunker Hill, 91
    Chancellorville, 47
    Chickamauga, 49
    Enchanted Rock, 32
    Eutaw Springs, 77
    Horseshoe Bend, 75
    Lexington and Concord, 90
    Little Big Horn, 41, 42

Monmouth, 29
New Orleans, 31
Princeton, 91
San Jacinto, 119
Shiloh, 49, 72
Slim Buttes, 42
Spotsylvania, 39
Trenton, 91
Wilderness, the, 39
Winchester (Second), 37
*Belfast News Letter*, 26
Belfast, Northern Ireland, 25, 27, 79, 91
*Belfast Telegraph*, 26
Bellaghy, Co Londonderry, 56-8
Benezet, Anthony, 113-6
Bernstein, Alice, 63
Biloxi, Mississippi, 49
*Blue Yodel (T for Texas)*, 70
Boston, Massachusetts, 29, 85, 86, 88, 90, 91, 92, 98, 99, 108, 109, 110, 117
Brewster, Elizabeth Morgan, 37
Brewster, William, 37
Bristol, England, 22, 50
Bristol, Tennessee/Virginia, 119, 120
Brunswick, Maine, 88
Bryant, James, 14
Bryant, Thomas Hoyt 'Slim', 70
Bryson, Rev JH, 15
Burlington, Iowa, 82
Burns, Robert, 12, 44-45, 100, 101, 103, 106

Calhoun, Vice President John C, 36
Calvert, Susan, 33

# INDEX

Cambridge, Massachusetts, 29, 93
Carothers, Wallace Hume, 82-4, *Section Two*
Carr, Leroy, 73
Carter Family, 70, 119, 120
Casco Bay, Maine, 88, 95, 98
Charleston, South Carolina, 20, 99
Chester County, South Carolina, 20, 117
Chicago, Illinois, 56, 60, 119
Churubusco, Mexico, 36, (34)
Clark, Rev Matthew, 86-87
Clinch River, Virginia, 120, (122)
Clinch Mountain Boys, 120
Civil War (American), 33, 37, 39, 40, 47, 49, 51, 76, 79, 80, 119, (122)
Coeburn, Virginia, 120
Coleraine, Co Londonderry, 85, 100, 109
Cody, William 'Buffalo Bill', 40, 41, 42
Conolly, William, MP, 65
Corrigan, Texas, 72, 73
Cotner, Carl, 70
Cotter, Joseph Seamon Jr, 54-55
Cotter, Joseph Seamon Sr, 53-55, *Section Two*
*Countess of Donegall, The* (barge), 26
Cowley, St Ledger, 50
Cowley, William, 50
Crawford, Captain Jack, 39-43, *Section One*
Crockett, David, 62, 121
Crudup, Arthur 'Big Boy', 77-78
Cunningham, Waddell, 25-26, *Section One*

Damariscotta River, Maine, 110, 111
Dandridge, Tennessee, 120
Darwin, Charles, 92
Daughters of the American Revolution (DAR), 80
Declaration of Independence, 28, 88
Delaware, Lackawanna and Western Railroad (DL&WR), 51
Derry, Pennsylvania, 31, 86
Derry, Northern Ireland, 19, 23, 31, 39, 43, 66, 90, 93, 102
Derry, Siege of, 85, 87, 102, 107
Detroit, Michigan, 35, 36, 81
Dickie, Anna Adams, 56-58
Dinsmoor, John, 100, 103-104
Dinsmoor, Robert, 100-107
Dominica, 26

Donegal, County, 31, 39, 72
Donelson, Rachel, 31
Dresden, Maine, 109
Dublin, Ireland, 22, 28, 35
Duffield, Rev George, 13-15, *Section One*
Dunbar, Colonel David, 9, 109-111
Dundy, Elaine, 75-76
Du Pont Company, 83-84

*East of Eden*, 66-67, 68
Early, Jubal, 37
Edwardes, Jonathan, 13- 95

Falmouth, Massachusetts, 9, 88, 95, 96, 97, 98
Flatt, Lester, 70
Foster, Stephen, 53
Fort,
    Frederick (also Pemaquid), 110, 111
    George, 100
    Haysboro, 31
    Houston, 120
    Knox, Kentucky, 92
    Knox, Maine, 92
    Laramie, 42
    Louisburg, 89, 90, 95
    McHenry, 30
    Ticonderoga, 92
    Washington, 29
Franklin, Benjamin, 23
Frazer, John Fries, 17-18, *Section One*

Galloway, William, 56
George I, King, 86
George III, King, 14
Georgia Wildcats, The, 70
Germantown, Philadelphia, 18, 23
Godfrey, Herbert, 58
Godfrey, Roley, 56
Godfrey, Thomas, 57
Gorham, Maine, 9, 96, 97, 98
Grand Old Opry, 73, 120
Grand Rapids, Michigan, 35, 37
Gray, Professor Asa, 92-93, *Section Two*
Great Hunger, The, 65
Great Wagon Road, The, 23, 79, 117
Greg, John, 25, 26
*Greg, The* (brig), 25
Greg, Thomas, 25-26, *Section One*
Gulf of St Lawrence, 50, 88

Haley, Bill, 73
Hamilton, Sir George of Greenlaw, 59
Hamilton, James, Earl of Abercorn, 59
Hamilton, Samuel, 65-67
Hays, John Coffee, 31-33, Section One
Hill, Wills, Colonial Secretary, 26
Houston, Sam, 31, 32, 119
Howe, General, 91, 92
Hudson Railroad, 51
Huguenot, 13, 16, 50, 59, 113
Hutcheson, Francis, 113, 115-116, Section Two

Jackson, General Thomas Jonathan 'Stonewall', 37, 119
*Jambalaya*, 73
James I, 65
*James and Mary, The* (emigrant ship), 20
Jefferson, 'Blind' Lemon, 73

Kearney, Phil, (34), 36
Kellogg, Rev Elijah, 9, 99, 97
Kennebec River, Maine, 9-10, 108, 109, 110
Kilgore, Robert, 120
Knox, General Henry, 91-92, Section Two
Koshkonong, Wisconsin, 56
Kyle, Mary, 58
Kyle, William, 58

Lafayette, General Marquis de, 29
Lawson, William, 120
Lewis, Jerry Lee, 73, 74
Lexington, Virginia, 119
Lima, Wisconsin, 56
Lisburn, Co Antrim, 25, 26, 46, 47, 48, 50, 51, 113
Lisburne, New York, 51
Liverpool, England, 28, 37, 98, 99
Log College, The, 23
Logan, James, 22-24, Section One
Logan, Patrick, 22
Logan, Sir Robert, 22
London, England, 22, 25, 28, 43, 81, 92, 111, 113
Londonderry, Northern Ireland, *see Derry, Northern Ireland*
Londonderry, New Hampshire, 85, 86, 87-88, 89, 90, 93, 100, 101, 102, 103, 104, 109, 110
*Look Homeward Angel*, 63

*Lord Hertford, The* (barge), 25
*Lord Dunluce, The* (emigrant ship), 20
Lough Neagh, Northern Ireland, 46, 58
Louisville, Kentucky, 15, 53, 54, 70, 71
Lurgan, Co Armagh, 22

MacMillin, John, 56, 57, 58
MacMillin, William, 58
Mansell, William, 75-76
Maple Grove Presbyterian Church, Virginia, 119
Martin, Rev William, 19-21, Section One
McCormick, Cyrus, 118-119
McCracken, Henry Joy, 27
McFadden, Andrew, 109
McGregor, James, 85-86, 90, 100, 102
McGregor, David, 87, 88, 106
McHenry, Daniel, 28
McHenry, James, 28-30, Section One
McKnight, Luke, 120
McLane, Senator Louis, 35
McLellan, Abigail, 97
McLellan, Bryce, 9, 95-96, 98, 99, Section Two
McLellan, Captain Joseph, 96, 97, 98, 99
McLellan, Captain William, 96, 97
McLellan, Deacon James, 96, 97
McLellan, Hugh, 96-97
McLellan, Stephen, 99
McLellan, Susannah, 96
McMichen, Clayton 'Mac' 'Pappy', 69-71, Section Two
McMullin, Mary Evalina, 82
McReynolds, General Andrew Thomas, 35-37, Section One
McReynolds, Frank, 37
McReynolds, Jesse, 120
McReynolds Tradition, The, 120
Merrymeeting Bay, 10, 109
Mexican War, 31, 32-3, 36, 76
Milwaukee, Wisconsin, 56, 57, 58
Mississippi, University of, 49
Moira, Co Down, 23, 24
Moira Presbyterian Church, 24
Monroe, Bill, 69
Montpelier, Maine, 92
Moody, Rev Samuel, 95
Morning Dove, 75-76
*Mountjoy, The* (merchant ship), 85, 102
Mulholland, Henry, 46, 47

# INDEX

Mulholland, Hugh, 46
Mulholland, Joseph Richardson Turtle, 47
Mulholland, General Sinclair, 46-7, *Section One*
Mulkeeragh, Ballykelly, 65-66, 67, *Section Two*
Mullican, Aubrey Wilson 'Moon', 72-74
Mullican, Oscar, 72
Mullican, Virginia, 72

Nashville, Tennessee, 31
*Neptune, The*, 114
Nesmith, James, 93
*New Jole Blon*, 73
New York (City), 25, 26, 29, 35, 43, 46-47, 48, 50, 51, 65, 77
New York University, 63
Nims, Frederick Augustine, 37

Oakland, California, 33
*Of Time and the River*, 63
Olaudau Equiano, 27
Old Kentucky Home, 62
Old Ripy Whiskey, 59-61

Patton, Elizabeth, 62
Patton, George, 62
Patton, Nancy, 62
Pejebscot Company, 108
Penn, William, 22-23, 113
Pennsylvania, University of, 16-18, 24
Petty, Sir William, 72
Philadelphia, Pennsylvania, 14, 15, 16, 17, 23, 24, 29, 40, 47, 60, 113, 117
Pigeon Forge, Tennessee, 121
Pittsburgh, Pennsylvania, 17, 35, 36
Pollock, Ann, 16
Portland, Maine, 95, 96, 98, 99
President (US),
    Adams, John, 14, 30, 89
    Cleveland, Grover, 80
    Clinton, Bill, 63
    Eisenhower, Dwight, 80, 81
    Harrison, William Henry, 36
    Jackson, Andrew, 31, 35, 36, 75
    Jefferson, Thomas, 99
    Kennedy, John F, 35, 80
    Lincoln, Abraham, 37
    Pierce, Franklin, 88
    Polk, James K, 36

Washington, George (General), 13, 15, 29, 30, 91, 92
Wilson, Woodrow, 80, 118
Presbyterian Church, 8, 9, 11, 13-15, 17, 20, 23, 26, 27, 51, 56, 57, 67, 80, 88, 95, 96, 105, 117
Presley, Elvis Aaron, 74, 75-78, *Section Two*
Presley, David, 77
Presley, Jessie Dee, 77
Presley, Vernon, 77
Presley, Gladys, 76
Princeton University, 13, 16, 23, 80
Puckett, Riley, 70

Quebec, Canada, 50, 90

Reeves, Jim, 73
Richburg, South Carolina, 20, 21
Rippey, Matthew, 59-60
Rippey, Nathan, 59-60
Rippy, William, 60
Ripy Brothers Distillery, 60
Ripy, Ernest, 60
Ripy, James, 60
Ripy, Joseph, 60
Ripy, Thomas B, 60
Ripy, Dr William, 59
*Robert* (brig), 86
Rodgers, Jimmie, 70, 73, 119
Rogers, Captain James, 88
Rogers, Major Robert, 88, 90
Rush, Dr Benjamin, 28, 114

Sagadahoc, Maine, 108, 110, 111
Sherman, General William T, 48, 49
Showboys, The, 73
Skillet Lickers, The, 69, 70
Sloan, Samuel, 50-52, *Section Two*
Sloane, Sir Hans, 113-115, 116
Smith, Bessie, 73
Society of the Cincinnati, 92
St Columb's Cathedral, Derry, Northern Ireland, 85, 102
Stark, Archibald, 90, 91
Stark, General John, 90-91, *Section Two*
State (US),
    Alabama, 76
    California, 31, 33, 43, 65, 66
    Delaware, 13, 28, 51
    Georgia, 69, 99

Illinois, 79, 80, 82, 83
Iowa, 82
Kentucky, 49, 53, 60, 62, 70, 71, 77, 79
Louisiana, 72
Maine, 7-10, 88, 90, 92, 95, 96, 98, 100, 102, 108, 109-110
Maryland, 13, 28, 29, 63, 72
Massachusetts, 9, 29, 85, 86, 88, 89, 92, 95, 98, 108, 109, 110, 111
Michigan, 35, 36, 37, 81
Mississippi, 31, 32, 76, 77, 119
Missouri, 77, 82
New Hampshire, 85, 86, 87, 88, 89, 90, 91, 93, 100, 102, 109, 110
New Jersey, 16, 17, 51, 70
New Mexico, 43
New York, *see also New York (City)*, 50, 51
North Carolina, 20, 49, 62, 75, 77, 79, 117
Ohio, 13, 23
Pennsylvania, 9, 13, 14, 16, 23, 28, 29, 31, 39, 40, 43, 79, 82, 109, 110, 117, 118
South Carolina, 19, 20, 21, 36, 75, 99, 117
Tennessee, 31, 48, 49, 72, 75, 78, 92, 119, 120, 121
Texas, 31, 32, 33, 70, 72, 73, 74, 119
Virginia, 13, 23, 29, 31, 80, 117, 118, 119, 120, (122)
West Virginia, (34)
Wisconsin, 56, 58
Staunton, Virginia, 118
Steinbeck, John, 65-68, 103
Stenton, Philadelphia, 23, *Section One*
Stevenson, Vice President Adlai Ewing I, 79-80, *Section Two*
Stevenson, Adlai Ewing II, 79, 80-81, *Section Two*
Stewart, Alexander Turney, 48
Stewart, Alexander Peter, 48-49, *Section Two*
Suffern, John, 50
Swan Island, 109
Sweetman, Helen, 84

Tar Heel, The, 63

Taylor, General Zachary, 32
Tazewell, Virginia, 119
Temple, Robert, 9, 108-109
Texas Rangers, 31, 32
Texas Playboys, The, 70, 73
Thomaston, Maine, 92
Thornton, Matthew, 88-89, *Section Two*
Travis, Merle, 70
Treaty of Paris, 26, 98
Tupelo, Mississippi, 75, 76, 77, 78
Tyrone, County, 35, 48, 59, 60, 110, 118, 119

University of Illinois, 82
University of North Carolina, 63
University of Pennsylvania, 16-18, 24

Vance, Francis, 57
Vaughn, Martha, 53
Virginia Boys, 120
Vow, The, Co Antrim, 19

Wade's Mill, Raphine, 118
War of Independence, *see American Revolutionary War*
Washington DC, 5, 70
Washington, Martha Dandridge, 120
Waters, Muddy, 77
Wells, Maine, 95
*When it's Peach Picking Time Down in Georgia*, 70, 71
Whitefield, Rev George, 13
Whittier, John Greenleaf, 103, 104
Wild Turkey Whiskey, 60
Williams, Hank, 73
Wills, Bob, 70, 73
Winchester, Tennessee, 48
Winchester, Virginia, 118
Winthrop, Colonel, 109
Wolfe, General, 90
Wolfe, Thomas Clayton, 62-63, *Section Two*
Woll, Adrian, 32
Wylie, Samuel Brown, 17, 18, 21, *Section One*

*You Can't Go Home Again*, 63